LEGAL PRAGMATISM

LEGAL PRAGMATISM

COMMUNITY, RIGHTS, AND DEMOCRACY

Michael Sullivan

Indiana University Press

BLOOMINGTON AND INDIANAPOLIS

This book is a publication of
Indiana University Press
601 North Morton Street
Bloomington, IN 47404-3797 USA

http://iupress.indiana.edu

Telephone orders 800-842-6796
Fax orders 812-855-7931
Orders by e-mail iuporder@indiana.edu

*The paper used in this publication meets the minimum
requirements of American National Standard for Information
Sciences—Permanence of Paper for Printed Library Materials,
ANSI Z39.48-1984.*

MANUFACTURED IN THE UNITED STATES OF AMERICA

Library of Congress Cataloging-in-Publication Data

Sullivan, Michael.
Legal pragmatism : community, rights, and democracy / Michael Sullivan.
p. cm.
Includes bibliographical references and index.
ISBN-13: 978-0-253-34887-6 (cloth)
ISBN-13: 978-0-253-21906-0 (pbk.)
1. Civil rights—United States. 2. Law—United States—Philosophy.
3. Civil rights—Philosophy. 4. Law—Philosophy. I. Title.
KF4749.S855 2007
342.7308'75—dc22
2006035466

1 2 3 4 5 12 11 10 09 08 07

For My Parents
shining exemplars, strong supporters, true friends

CONTENTS

ACKNOWLEDGMENTS

The list of intellectual debts I've incurred in writing this book is long and I am sure there are many who deserve mention that will slip through this final accounting. Without the criticism, advice, and encouragement of many colleagues, teachers, mentors, friends, and students, this book would not have come into being. I am confident the final product is much better for their wisdom and generosity of spirit.

John Lysaker has been my single most important philosophical interlocutor through more than a decade. His genius at seeing the big picture has helped me find coherence when I had become lost in the details. John Stuhr has the sharpest, most penetrating critical eye and the highest demands of any reader I have ever encountered. His criticisms have provoked more and better responses though never quite as much as they merited. Daniel Solove, the coauthor of the article which contained an earlier version of chapter 3, has been my intellectual companion in legal theory since my first days at Yale Law School. What started as my attempt to teach him a little philosophy has become an ongoing conversation on law in which my judgments have been routinely altered by his far-reaching insights.

In addition to these central influences, I am grateful to John Lachs, who models the virtues, seeks to empower seemingly everyone he meets, and by example shows the way to a stronger community. His comments and observations saved me from many mistakes. Charles Scott helped slow down my approach to philosophical thinking at a time when the pressures were uniformly encouraging only speed. The result has been deeper and richer than it would have been otherwise.

Many professors at the Yale Law School provided intellectual guidance and inspiration, including Bruce Ackerman, Jack Balkin, Reva Siegel, Tony Kronman, Owen Fiss, Harold Koh, Guido Calabresi, and Charles Reich. Among these, Bruce Ackerman stands out for his rare ability to take criticism in the spirit it is given and respond in kind, encouraging robust exchange on heated topics without sacrificing mutual respect.

A number of friends from outside the academy have continued to offer critical assistance and a helpful reality check on my ideas. Their shared commitment to making a better community sustains hope even in dark times. These include Terry McInnis, Shawn Collins, Nate Johnson, Todd Brown, Mary Kamb, and Tom Robinson.

Finally, among the most important debts are those to my colleagues and students at Emory University. Cindy Willett, Rudolf Makkreel, and Steven Strange of the Philosophy Department read large portions of the manuscript and offered valuable suggestions. Robert Schapiro, Michael Perry, and Timothy Terrell of the law school, in addition to members of the legal theory workshop, made significant critical contributions. My undergraduate and graduate students in courses on American philosophy, philosophy of law, and pragmatism endured trial runs of several hypotheses and never failed to ask probing questions which made me reconsider my conclusions.

For this abundance of criticism and intellectual support, I am grateful.

LEGAL PRAGMATISM

Introduction

In this book, I develop and set forth a pragmatic theory of rights in the context of a larger account of American law, judicial review, and democracy. My theory of rights is pragmatic in two important senses. First, it draws deeply on the pragmatism of classical American philosophers such as Charles Peirce, William James, and, above all, John Dewey. Second, it seeks to reconstruct the critical resources of this pragmatic philosophy to improve not just our legal theories but, above all, our legal practices—especially those which concern the scope of legal rights, the process of judicial review, and conflicts between individual and community interests.

This is a large, important, and timely issue because of deep disagreements about these matters in American society coupled with intellectual paralysis about how to resolve these disagreements in intelligent ways. We are, for example, awash in the rhetoric of rights and in particular affirmations and denials of rights—from the right to health care or prescription drugs to the right to choice in public schooling; from the right to marriage and civil union to the right to a living wage;

from the rights of citizenship to the rights of illegal immigrants; and from the rights of our government in times of war and terror to the rights of prisoners. These issues are crucial, but we do not have a clear, critical, effective way to think about and respond to them. These same problems mark judicial review, the authority of the Supreme Court (or other courts) to review duly enacted laws and to strike them down when they violate provisions of the Constitution, such as the Bill of Rights. In the United States, courts may have this authority or power, but when is it legitimate or warranted to exercise this power? This question arises across a wide range of cases from affirmative action to the USA Patriot Act and from eminent domain to assisted suicide. Here too we lack a coherent, useful philosophical account of our practices and their alternatives. Finally, disagreements and disputes between individual interests and community interests are at a fever pitch. Battles over gun ownership and its restrictions, campus speech codes, zoning and property use laws, the privacy of communications, tax breaks for private corporations and companies, and the role of religion in politics and the public sphere are just a few of the many examples. In these cases, how are we to understand community, individualism, and the value and place of each within democracy?

Any attempt to set forth a pragmatic theory of rights must begin with the roadblocks that obviously confront it. The first of these is the philosophy of communitarianism, a philosophy that in its several forms insists that any central focus on individualism and individual rights is a vestige of an outdated liberalism that now only undermines community interest and the real development of democracy in the United States. Communitarians ask a compelling question: Why should the rights of a lone individual trump the interests of the state or larger community? The communitarians claim that this focus on rights inevitably favors the individual over the community and allows able or lucky individuals to pursue their own private ends at the expense of the good of the community. This criticism has had a significant impact on rights far beyond the realm of those who identify themselves as communitarian.

After setting forth the communitarian view, I demonstrate in chapter 1 how it depends upon an untenable dichotomy between the individual and the community. It turns out upon closer scrutiny that concern with community not only *is* compatible with concern for individual rights, but also that concern with community actually requires concern for individual rights and development of a theory of rights. Pragmatism, since its inception, has undermined this community/individual dichotomy, along with many other dichotomies and dualisms.

The results of chapter 1 immediately bring into focus a second major roadblock that confronts any pragmatic account of rights and law—the commonplace but mistaken view that pragmatism is inconsistent with rights. Many liberal theorists—most notably and most influentially legal theorist and philosopher Ronald Dworkin—have sought to answer the communitarian challenge and explain why an individual should prevail on claims of right against the state. They've focused especially on cases involving rights of free speech, free assembly, freedom of religion, privacy, and other cases which pit the "individual" against an array of government interests. They've argued that rights are best understood as trumps that an individual may use in special cases to block social policy even when that policy is designed to promote the best future for the community. As a result of this analysis, however, they've concluded that pragmatism, committed as it is to seeking the best future, must be hostile to rights. In chapter 2, I debunk this assertion and show in detail that these arguments which typically drive a wedge between rights and pragmatism fail and that, contrary to such impressions, pragmatism offers the most compelling and coherent justification for a theory of rights. It does this by recognizing the crucial role rights play in creating conditions necessary for individuals to flourish and receive fair treatment.

Having undermined the communitarian skepticism about rights and Dworkin's liberal skepticism about pragmatism, in the third chapter I am ready to sketch the central features of a pragmatic account of rights, law, and democracy. However, there is one final roadblock to this project which first must be cleared—the recent attempts to cast pragmatism as an unambitious and inherently conservative common-sense doctrine. Indeed, as a result of the prevalence of these attempts, pragmatism about rights and law now suffers as much from its self-identified friends as it does from its outspoken enemies.

For example, Thomas Grey, the Stanford law professor whose essays championed pragmatism at the dawn of its recent renaissance,[1] has written that a "pragmatist theory of law is, like much pragmatist theory, essentially banal."[2] Meanwhile Richard Rorty, the philosopher often credited as much as anyone with reviving pragmatism, concurs.[3] For Grey and Rorty, pragmatism is banal because it "is the implicit working theory of most good lawyers."[4] Rorty writes: "Pragmatism was reasonably shocking seventy years ago, but in the ensuing decades it has gradually been absorbed into American common sense."[5] Most visible on political and legal issues among these "friends," however, is the prolific writer Richard Posner.

Pragmatism could not ask for a more influential spokesperson. As Ronald Dworkin has noted, "Richard Posner is the wonder of the legal world." He is a judge on the highly visible Seventh Circuit Court of Appeals, a senior lecturer at the University of Chicago Law School, and one of the most frequently cited legal scholars of our age.[6] Thus Posner naturally occupies a position at the forefront of legal debates, and he has rapidly become the steward of an account of law which he identifies as pragmatism. He proclaims that "pragmatism is the best description of the American judicial ethos";[7] it is "[n]ebulous and banal, modest and perhaps even timorous—or maybe oscillating unpredictably between timorous and bold."[8]

While Posner's project is in part well-intended—he too seeks to defend pragmatism against liberal critics like Dworkin—its core is not well-conceived either in its conclusions or its ambitions. Posner dismisses philosophy as "intellectual pretension" and chooses to view ideals as useless and philosophical theorizing as empty. In chapter 3, I show how this version of pragmatism has been stripped of any power for critical cultural reconstruction. Without any meaningful way to evaluate social goals, Posner's account of pragmatism devolves into an efficiency exercise on behalf of unexamined values. The point of this exercise becomes merely finding appropriate means to achieve given ends. While this search for means may take a deliberative form, Posner's account has little to say about the critical selection of ends. Ironically, his attack on abstract ideals becomes, in effect, an endorsement of such ideals, since it leaves unreconstructed the dominant, often unexamined and self-unaware ideals of present society. Because of the ways Posner aligns himself with common sense and against any use of moral and political theory, and the way he champions efficiency over other social values, Posner's pragmatism ends up with no critical edge and little ability to address intelligently the very kinds of debates that gave rise to this theorizing in the first place.

With this background, and with the clearing away of these major roadblocks, in chapter 4 I present my own critical account of pragmatism and explain the reconstruction it makes possible. Drawing on Dewey and a conception of pragmatism as reconstructive (rather than, say, Richard Rorty and a conception of pragmatism as merely deflationary), this view highlights the ways pragmatism subjects values and ideals to the tests of experience and practice. The fact that experience is not governed by timeless, fixed absolutes does not render either critical reflection or our ideals baseless and unrooted. It means instead that we must be willing to bring our ideals and values back down to earth, to recognize their origins in past experience, and to subject them to criticism and reconstruction as we employ them in the present under changed circumstances.

To illustrate concretely the nature of this pragmatic account of rights and law, I turn to the problem of judicial review in chapter 5. The problem is posed this way: How are individual rights to be protected in practice? More specifically, when courts protect individual rights under the Constitution, as the legal scholar Alexander Bickel recognized when he dubbed this the counter-majoritarian difficulty, they often do so by voiding laws that were passed according to democratic processes. As a result, this practice by the courts raises questions of legitimacy because the judges who make these decisions are not elected whereas the laws they invalidate have been passed democratically by elected representatives. Rights that are claimed in theory but that do not work in practice are, from a pragmatic perspective, not rights at all because the process of protecting them undermines the reciprocity between individual and community essential for democracy. The pragmatic reconstruction of this difficulty reconceives the nature of democracy and explains how the judiciary is well-suited through judicial review to extend rather than undermine democracy. In the end, a pragmatic reconstruction of law and an expansion of democracy are seen to walk hand in hand.

ONE

What's Right with Rights and Wrong with Communitarianism?

We are different and we don't know exactly why. And this is America,
where the rights of the minority are protected.
—Erin Wiser, *Los Angeles Times*

Seventeen-year-old Erin Wiser belonged to the "Gay/Straight Alliance," a club started at her high school by a fellow student so that
students could talk to each other about sexual identity. This innovative
club was not well-received, however, by the Salt Lake City Board of
Education. They voted to ban the club.[1] In fact, the board voted to ban
all extracurricular clubs, including the chess, Latino, Frisbee, and Bible
clubs. Since the board was concerned that an order to ban only the
Gay/Straight Alliance might not survive a constitutional challenge of
viewpoint discrimination, they decided to ban every extracurricular
club.[2] State Senator Charles Stewart expressed the prevailing political
sentiment: "I think this is such a threat to our society, our children and
our families that if the only way to keep these clubs from organizing is
to ban all clubs, I'll vouch for that."[3]

It is surprising that a high school club, with a mere sixteen members, is capable of threatening our whole society, but Senator Stewart
talks as if the horrifying nature of this threat is patently obvious. Ms.
Wiser, in her statement, emphasizes that although the individuals in

her club are "different," they belong to a country that protects "difference" and protects minorities from political pressure to conform.[4] In her view, Senator Stewart's concern for "civilization" represents a threat not only to her student club, but also to America's pluralistic democracy.

This particular debate is symbolic of a larger struggle presently taking place in American society. As Ms. Wiser and her friends are exploring questions of self-identity, so too is America. Politicians on the far right, such as Patrick Buchanan, have described their cause as the "taking back of America."[5] They believe that the once-great American identity has been splintered by disruption of traditional institutions, such as the family, and an increasing willingness to confer legitimacy upon "inappropriate" lifestyles, such as homosexuality.[6] On the left, worries abound that traditional institutions, particularly our schools, now languish in chaos. The Clinton administration supported widespread drug testing in schools, and President Clinton lobbied for school uniforms in his 1996 State of the Union address.[7]

One might be tempted to dismiss such events as "politics as usual," but upon closer inspection, it appears that what is "usual" is changing. There is a palpable sense in the present political dialogue that our grand tradition of protecting individual rights is interfering ever more with our ability to construct a well-ordered society. If we cannot protect such symbols of national unity as the flag from public desecration, it is asked, how can we expect to build or even maintain a community? If, as a nation, we are incapacitated by the Supreme Court from pronouncing on the substantive human goods embodied in prohibiting abortion and promoting heterosexual marriage, then it must not be any surprise that our communities remain fragmented. Under such circumstances, individuals are left to float adrift without secure objects of moral and emotional attachment by which to orient their social lives.

Under the weight of such concern, there has been an explosion of sociopolitical literature. At the popular level, books like *The Moral Compass* by William Bennett[8] and *The Closing of the American Mind* by Allan Bloom[9] have sought to provide direction toward these objects of moral attachment. Bennett's compilation emphasizes the importance of early education in the formation of a strong moral character informed with conservative virtues, whereas Bloom seeks to recover a discourse of truth for a system of higher education that has been swallowed in the sea of relativism. Both authors subscribe to a version of the thesis that the good life, for individuals, is a function of their participation in the larger community. Joining them in this regard are several members of the left who champion "communitarianism" over what they see as the radical individualism of the present. These writers, like Mary Ann Glendon and Michael J. Sandel, believe that liberalism has gone too far down the path of protecting individuals in their choice of a conception of the good life. As a result, society now finds itself unable to make thoughtful, deliberative choices concerning which substantive human goods the community as a whole will pursue.[10]

> In our investigation of American rights talk, we have observed a tendency to formulate important issues in terms of rights; a bent for stating rights claims in a stark, simple, and absolute fashion; an image of the rights-bearer as radically free, self-determining, and self-sufficient; and the absence of well-developed responsibility talk.[11]

Professor Glendon believes that focusing on individual rights tends to reinforce an atomistic view of individuality. Instead of fostering dialogue and dispute resolution, she believes the invocation of rights tends to drive individuals apart and destroy the conditions for community. Professor Sandel offers a related critique, claiming that respect for rights has come to mean that the state must remain neutral with respect to any conception of the good life in order not to infringe upon the autonomy of individuals in making their choices. As a result of this neutrality requirement, the larger community is prevented from making decisions to direct community life toward the realization of substantive goods.[12]

In this chapter, I want to take issue with both the descriptive and prescriptive claims advanced by communitarians. First, I will challenge the view that American history is properly characterized as exalting the individual's rights over community aims. On the contrary, much of the case law, which ardently articulates our American commitment to individual rights, renders decisions for the "community" rather than the individual. Consider the potential litigation in Ms. Wiser's case. If the issue is framed as a choice between the individual rights of these students to organize and discuss their sexuality versus a community interest in protecting and preserving society, then the students will face a heavy, perhaps insurmountable, burden. The irony, in my view, is that the "rights talk" Glendon finds so prevalent in modern society is not a reflection of the overabundance of strong rights enjoyed by individuals, but a response to the perceived lack of such rights that manifests itself in vocal expression. Second, I will argue that the proper response to recognition of the precariousness of individuals in modern society is not weaker rights for individuals, but stronger rights. It is true that our older credos of individualism are out of step with the times in which we live. It no longer makes sense, if it ever did, to reduce individual freedom to a simple postulate of preventing governmental intrusion into private life. But communitarians focus chiefly upon the ways allegiance to such a postulate prevents the realization of substantive goods through community action. There are also worries that our "older" individualism hinders individuals in their quest for growth and self-realization. I will try to show why I think this concern is misplaced in the present debate. Contrary to communitarian belief, we need stronger rights to support the growth of individuals.

REALITY ABOUT RIGHTS

Underlying the assertion that our present discourse is dominated by rights talk is the charge that an absolutist and abstract doctrine of individual rights has held sway over the American legal tradition. Glendon offers the following description of this malevolent social force:

> The most distinctive features of our American rights dialect are . . . : its penchant for absolute, extravagant formulations, its near-aphasia concerning responsibility, its excessive homage to individual independence and self-sufficiency, its habitual concentration on the individual and state at the expense of the intermediate groups of civil society, and its unapologetic insularity. Not only does each of these traits make it difficult to give voice to common sense or moral intuitions, they also impede development of the sort of rational political discourse that is appropriate to the needs of a mature, complex, liberal, pluralistic republic.[13]

I agree with Glendon that one can find many a formulation of individual rights in Supreme Court cases that have an absolutist ring to them. However, next to many of these formulations one finds decisions vindicating not the individual but the government. Indeed, Glendon herself explores the ineffectiveness of invoking individual property rights in the context of protecting a Michigan Polish community from the bulldozer. The call to preserve the uniqueness of that historical community was no match for the "public use" interest in replacing the community with a new Cadillac plant.[14]

This result is not unusual in cases in which individual rights are confronted with public interests, even when those rights stem from absolutist language.[15] Even the First Amendment seems to eliminate any gray area:

> Congress shall make no law respecting an establishment of religion, or prohibiting the free exercise thereof; or abridging the freedom of speech, or of the press, or the right of the people peaceably to assemble and to petition the Government for a redress of grievances.[16]

Indeed, the most well-known feature of Justice Hugo Black's jurisprudence was his insistence on the absolute character of the First Amendment's prohibition against abridging speech.[17] But consider the case of Anita Whitney's conviction under the California Criminal Syndicate Act.[18] This act made it a crime to knowingly join an organization that urged unlawful means to accomplish political change. Ms. Whitney attended the national convention of the Socialist Party and advocated seeking socialist ends through political processes of the time. A harder line was adopted by the convention, however, and Ms. Whitney was subsequently convicted under the Syndicate Act for knowingly maintaining her membership in that group.

The question of the case is whether an individual's membership in a group constitutes a criminal act when the group advocates against prevailing laws. What is Ms. Whitney's interest in this case? The appellate record provides scant details. Ms. Whitney wanted to join the political organization of her choice. This group, the Socialist Party, decided that the greater ends of the Party warranted extralegal means. Ms. Whitney disagreed but did not resign her membership. She wanted to continue to participate, not in violence, theft, or terrorism, but simply in the continuing dialogue of the party. If we allow such political activity to be criminalized, then we close the door to political expression to those who do not hold majority views. And, as Erin Wiser noted above, our self-proclaimed American tradition prides itself on protection of minorities.

What is the interest of the state of California? The state was worried that advocacy of disregarding prevailing law in pursuit of socialist goals would be successful. That is, the concern was that such advocacy would lead to increased lawlessness that would threaten state security. What happens when these two sets of interests are weighed against one another?

In response to this case, Justice Brandeis refused to recognize mere advocacy against law as grounds for criminalization. While he admits that "every denunciation of existing law tends in some measure to increase the probability that there will be violation of it," he also insists that only imminent and serious evils ought to warrant interference with free speech and association. This sounds like a strenuous hurdle for legislation to surmount, but legislatures elected by majorities, like those in Utah and Orange County, California, are apt to view individual perceptions in competition with majority predispositions as serious evils. Consider Senator Stewart's view of the sixteen-person Gay/Straight Alliance—an evil that threatens our entire society.[19]

Something is amiss in the structure of Brandeis' text. It says that legislatures can pass laws infringing speech only when they are seeking to prevent a serious evil. Imagine a similar law along search-and-seizure lines. The legislature may authorize police searches of homes which infringe individual rights to privacy only when they are seeking to prevent a serious evil. This limitation offers little protection to individuals because the legislature is almost always seeking to prevent a serious evil to the general welfare when it passes such legislation. The rub is that in doing so, it often inflicts such evils upon individuals.

The brilliance of Brandeis was his recognition that we must clarify the relation of the individual to the state if we are to make progress in resolving this dispute. His well-known attempt not only privileges the individual—much to the chagrin of communitarians, one may suppose[20]—but also ties that privileging to a conception of democracy that depends on empowering individuals:

> Those who won our independence believed that the final end of the state was *to make men free to develop their faculties;* and that in its government the deliberative forces should prevail over the arbitrary. They valued liberty both as an end and as a means. They believed liberty to be the secret of happiness and courage to be the secret of

liberty. They believed that freedom to think as you will and to speak as you think are means indispensable to the discovery and spread of political truth; that without free speech and assembly discussion would be futile; that with them, discussion affords ordinarily adequate protection against the dissemination of noxious doctrine; that the greatest menace to freedom is an inert people; that public discussion is a political duty; and that this should be a fundamental principle of the American government.[21]

The goal of a society is to make obtaining fulfillment possible for individuals, and society discovers the methods to do so through dialogue amongst individuals. Thus the United States must protect individual expression both as an end of its central mission to help individuals grow and as a means to the ongoing (re)formation of a society that can best empower individual growth. No doubt this is a complicated affair in a pluralistic society, with many competing accounts of the good life proffered, but it provides a starting point for analysis. It reminds us that even when our personal views agree with the majority on a particular subject, our democratic ideals are tarnished and our practice impoverished by exclusion of minority viewpoints.

In the context of the communitarian debate, two points are salient: First, any attempt to curtail the right of Ms. Whitney to associate with the political group of her choice (presuming she is not engaged in illegal behavior) undercuts the preconditions for democratic life. Thus one may believe that protection of Ms. Whitney's individual rights is in accordance with, not counter to, protecting the community's democratic aspirations. More importantly, such laws deny individuals the opportunity to become whomever they want to become by replacing their own choices with the paternalistic preferences of the state.

Second, although this passage by Brandeis, in which democracy's commitment to the individual is celebrated, is famous, the actual holding of the Court went against Ms. Whitney. Thus, counter to what communitarians would lead us to believe, we find, even in the most celebrated defenses of rights, a predominance of rights talk but an absence of rights. This is even more apparent in the majority opinion, written by Justice Sanford, which had an altogether different tone. The majority was not interested in Ms. Whitney's interests, but only the extent of legislative power in light of First Amendment doctrine. Sanford concluded: "a State in the exercise of its police power may punish those who abuse [the freedom of speech] by utterances inimical to the public welfare, tending to incite crime, disturb the peace, or endanger the foundations of organized government and threaten its overthrow by unlawful means." Ms. Whitney was imprisoned because she chose to belong to the wrong political party, a party whose utterances were "inimical to the public welfare."

On some accounts of liberalism, the Court's conclusion is wrong because it is not neutral between conceptions of the good life.[22] That is, it favors democracy over socialism. Michael Sandel, however, considers the liberal response misguided.[23] He contends that content neutrality is the wrong aspiration. Rather, he suggests that the Court must recognize the limits of the "procedural republic" and confront the truth that it is "not always possible to adjudicate rights without passing judgment on the morality of the cause they would advance."[24] Sandel is right that content neutrality is often the wrong aspiration, but insisting that courts pass judgment on the morality of the cause they would advance is hardly a helpful injunction because the question in each case is about which cause is to be advanced. Would protecting Ms. Whitney's speech rights enhance individual self-expression and exploration in the political realm, or would it advance socialism? Courts need a principle for distinguishing between causes, and here they should follow Brandeis' advice and privilege those causes that empower individuals to choose for themselves. As Emerson reminds us, democracy involves a commitment to the idea that individuals should judge for themselves. Admittedly, there will still be debate over which decisions empower and disempower individuals, but that end—and not deference to the larger community—should function to guide our discussions.

The words of Brandeis' concurrence are remembered, but *Whitney's* legacy of capitulation to the community is repeated in administrative regulation of individual behavior in other contexts.[25] Before I explore these, I want to emphasize a specific point contrary to the communitarian suggestions that rights of an absolute character have run amok in our political landscape. No right reads more absolutely than the First Amendment, but the circumstances under which that right has been understood to apply in full force have been restricted to speakers participating in public debate on the question of America's political constitution. The explanation for this selective application is that the maintenance of democracy as a process of collective self-formation requires that our public debate remain free from external coercion.[26] Speech in other contexts, however, such as in school and at work, which have not been understood to be related to our public discourse on political identity, has received substantially less protection. Professor Robert Post provides an explanation for this differentiation in his book *Constitutional Domains:*

> Managerial structures necessarily presuppose objectives that are unproblematic and hence that can be used instrumentally to regulate domains of social life. The enterprise of public discourse, by contrast, rests on the value of collective autonomy, which requires that all possible objectives, all possible versions of national identity, be rendered problematic and open to inquiry. No particular objective can justify the coercive censorship of public discourse without simultaneously contradicting the very enterprise of self-determination.[27]

The upshot of Post's analysis is that while government must establish a compelling state interest to overcome a First Amendment assertion of right in a case such as Ms. Whitney's, a burden that was met more easily than one might expect, the government need only show that speech in the managerial/administrative realm interferes with the goal of the managerial enterprise to warrant its regulation. Thus, in the face of overwhelming expansion of administrative law, one now finds in practice anything but the rampant proliferation of absolute rights forecast by communitarians.

In school, for instance, children learn from history and social studies to respect the vocabulary of individual rights. At the same time, however, they often learn from experience that these rights are not competitive when placed head-to-head with the instrumental goals of the educational institution. Although schools are allowed to forbid rights-protected conduct only when they can show "that engaging in the forbidden conduct would 'materially and substantially interfere with the requirements of appropriate school discipline in the operation of the school,' "[28] the Court has been willing to grant school administrations considerable discretion in interpreting these standards.[29] The Court's deference stems in part from the idea that school is a managerial activity, not an exercise in democratic public discourse.[30] But what lessons do children learn about the role of individualism in the application of such standards? What kind of example has the Court been setting in its treatment of students?

In 1983, Matt Fraser gave the following speech at his high school government nominating convention:

> I know a man who is firm—he's firm in his pants, he's firm in his shirt, his character is firm—but most . . . of all, his belief in you, the students of Bethel is firm. Jeff Kuhlman is a man who takes his point and pounds it in. If necessary he'll take an issue and nail it to the wall. He doesn't attack things in spurts—he drives hard, pushing and pushing until finally—he succeeds. Jeff is a man who will go to the very end—even the climax, for each and every one of you. So vote for Jeff for A.S.B. vice-president—he'll never come between you and the best our high school can be.[31]

As punishment for this evocative speech, Mr. Fraser was suspended from school for three days and prohibited from speaking at graduation. He filed a lawsuit in district court requesting an injunction against the punishment, which was granted and later affirmed by the Ninth Circuit Court of Appeals. The Supreme Court granted certiorari and reversed the decision. Chief Justice Burger, writing for the majority, sought to balance Mr. Fraser's individual interest in expression against the public interest in teaching students proper social decorum.

> The undoubted freedom to advocate unpopular and controversial views in schools and classrooms must be balanced against the society's countervailing interest in teaching students the boundaries of socially appropriate behavior.[32]

It is interesting to note that there is nothing in the record to indicate that Mr. Fraser's speech was unpopular, though it was obviously controversial to the administration. The administration stressed its *Tinker* interest in avoiding disruptions that would otherwise hinder the educational process.[33] Chief Justice Burger accepted this but was more impressed with the thought that administrations should be able to punish students who exhibit socially inappropriate behavior because such behavior serves as an example to other students.

> The process of educating our youth for citizenship in public schools is not confined to books, the curriculum, and the civics class; schools

must teach by example the shared values of a civilized social order. Consciously or otherwise, teachers—and indeed the older students—demonstrate the appropriate form of civil discourse and political expression by their conduct and deportment in and out of class. Inescapably, like parents, they are role models. The schools, as instruments of the state, may determine that the essential lessons of civil, mature conduct cannot be conveyed in a school that tolerates lewd, indecent, or offensive speech and conduct such as that indulged in by this *confused* boy.[34]

Chief Justice Burger had little to say concerning Mr. Fraser's interest. What little worry is evinced concerning prohibiting individual expression is dismissed with the claim that children's rights to free expression are less extensive than those of adults.[35] No thought is given to lesser restrictive methods of redressing the perceived harm, such as greater dialogue with students. Indeed, when a teacher chose to spend some class time discussing the speech with students, such time was treated as pure disruption. To his credit, Chief Justice Burger does ask which course of action will help the students develop, but his emphasis is not on the development of their individual faculties, as Brandeis urges in his *Whitney* concurrence, but on bringing student behavior into conformity with socially sanctioned standards.

We can see this same impulse at work in a variety of other cases in the school setting. In his 1996 State of the Union address, President Clinton endorsed adopting a school uniform policy for public school students. Similar policies have been championed on the grounds that they reduce gang-related violence in the schools.[36] In 1987, Daryll Olesen was suspended from his high school for wearing an earring. The school administration found that Mr. Olesen's earring wearing violated the school board's policy prohibiting the wearing of gang symbols, although the policy did not mention earrings explicitly. The rationale for the policy was to deter gang-related violence, and the principal of the high school testified that the policy achieved its aim. Mr. Olesen denied that his earring was in any way meant to signify gang affiliation, contending instead that his jewelry expressed his individuality and was attractive to the opposite sex.[37] Although the Court was skeptical that Mr. Olesen had no gang affiliations, it decided to give him the "benefit of the doubt."[38]

The Court began its discussion of the law by noting that it is the "responsibility [of the school board] to teach not only English and History, but the role of young men and women in our democratic society. Students learn to think and to question. But students are also expected to learn the rules which govern their behavior not only in school but in society."[39] Citing *Fraser,* the Court held that it is up to the school board to prescribe the "direction and manner of this instruction."[40]

Although it is true as a matter of established law that restrictions in the service of the educational mission, which could not survive constitutional scrutiny outside of the schooling context, may be tolerated, the Court in *Olesen* expected students to learn their proper role in democratic society through submission to dress code requirements that facilitate administrative attempts to curb violence in schools. The lesson seems apropos, however, only to the extent that one assumes individuals in democratic society should habituate themselves to giving up opportunities for individual expression when doing so makes the task of administrative agencies easier. It might make more sense to teach participants in the democratic process to demand that individuals both be allowed to choose their own dress and be protected from the threat of gang violence. Unfortunately, the Court chose a different path and refused to find any infringement on a First Amendment right to self-expression in Mr. Olesen's case.

> Olesen claims that the school's anti-gang policy which includes a prohibition against males wearing earrings violates his right of free speech and expression. We disagree. In order to claim the protection of the First Amendment, Olesen must demonstrate that his conduct intended "to convey a particularized message . . . and . . . the likelihood [is] great that the message would be understood by those who viewed it." Olesen's only message is one of his "individuality." In order to send that message, he is willing to violate school rules designed to protect him and his fellow students. We find that his "message" is not within the protected scope of the First Amendment.[41]

Since the Court found no infringement of a fundamental right, the school board's policy is subjected to a lenient, rational-basis review. Even if the Court had found a First Amendment interest on Mr. Olesen's behalf, the *Tinker* precedent and the *Fraser* holding, discussed above, allow restrictions when necessary for the successful operation of the schooling process.

The crucial question is this: What does the phenomenon of gang violence in school make necessary? Does it make necessary the adoption of dress codes, or is there a less restrictive alternative to the problem of reducing gang violence? After a lengthy description of Mr. Olesen's declining high school performance, Judge Plunkett concluded: "Daryll Olesen may yet fulfill the promise he once showed. If he does, perhaps it will be aided by his lesson here."[42] If courts refuse to make inquiries into the policies of administrative bodies, what lesson will students learn? At the very least, students will know they must not risk expression, which the administration may later frown upon. They may further understand that their self-expression is not a candidate for serious protection because such protection proves detrimental to the public interest in teaching them how to become good citizens. The problem with this formulation—and it is a central problem with the communitarian thesis I will explore below—is that individuals are put in the service of community, and scant attention is spent discovering how communities might help release the capacities of individuals for their own self-realization. One might respond that the development of community is a more important goal than facilitating individual growth, but one cannot ignore how the two goals are intertwined. Maintenance of a vital community requires individuals with a deep capacity for understanding problems and creative resources for addressing them. To develop students' understanding, however, the educational process must consider how to engage, rather than exclude, each student's individual interests. This was the conclusion John Dewey reached after his extensive investigation of the educational process:

> One of the chief causes for failure in school to secure that gain in ability to understand that is a precious educational result is the neglecting to set up the conditions for active use as a means in bringing consequences to pass—the neglecting to provide projects that call out the inventiveness and ingenuity of pupils in proposing aims to realize, or finding means to realize, consequences already thought of. All routine and all externally dictated activity fail to develop ability to understand, even though they promote skill in external doing.[43]

Of course, a commitment to engaging student interests need not proscribe adoption of a dress code, but the inquiry deserves broader attention than the Court gave it here. There is instead considerable emphasis on protecting the ability of the educational process to develop democratic citizens, with little analysis of whether the process succeeds. Perhaps one should investigate the problem from a different perspective and consider how well the environment of the schoolhouse prepares students for the environment of the workforce.[44] Because we live in a country where many individuals are forced to take jobs that engage them at a level far below their abilities,[45] perhaps a schooling policy that fails to develop individual capacities should be pursued. Ironically, by underdeveloping the capacities of individuals, they may be better able to cope with the routine and mechanical work that constitutes such a high proportion of available jobs. Indeed, such an approach would lessen the pain produced by the difference between individual expectations for job satisfaction and actual job satisfaction. Of course, educating individuals to accept boredom and conformity in the workplace is entirely inimical to the American commitment Brandeis identified as educating individuals into their full potentiality, but it is a disturbing thought that our present regime might be better at the former than at the latter.

In a perceptive passage, William Arrowsmith argued that one cannot develop Druids by offering rewards for Druid of the Year.[46] If you want Druids, you need to have forests. I think the same is true of democracy: One cannot make democratic citizens by teaching democratic principles through authoritarian pedagogy. If we teach the rhetoric of rights in schools but practice a form of authoritarianism, it is little wonder that this separation between rhetoric and lived experience is reproduced in the larger social sphere. Students are tested more on what they write than on how they act. They internalize one set of answers for exam questions about democracy and individual rights but live under very different conditions, learning incompatible lessons from their most significant role models.

We live in a country with a strong commitment to individualism and individual rights. And it is precisely the verbal manifestation of this commitment that leads thinkers like Glendon to lament the pervasiveness of rights talk. However, in the context of the rights we've explored, one sees not the triumph of individuals but their subordination to administrative interests. The problem isn't just systemic incoherence, though. Without protecting the spheres within which individuals are able to explore and experiment with their sense of self, no society will be able to facilitate the growth of its citizens.

Presently, we participate in a culture in which administrative organizations representing the "public interest" are allowed to dismiss the claims of individuals as hazy, ephemeral, or just plain insignificant in the context of the greater good. It is this situation, not the proliferation of rights talk, that poses the most serious threat to the well-being of society. Therefore, in order to address the challenges confronting us, we must reconsider how best to secure spheres of individual freedom and self-determination. It is my contention that greater attention to rights, understood pragmatically, can contribute to developing an alternative to this deepening administrative quagmire.

RETHINKING RIGHTS FOR THE PRESENT: SHOULD WE BE "PRAGMATIC" ABOUT RIGHTS?

Ask any American what makes America great, and they are likely to mention the virtues of democracy, respect for individual rights, and economic opportunity. These themes have endured. Indeed, they are all present in the Declaration of Independence, which marks our birth as a free and sovereign nation.

> WE hold these Truths to be self-evident, that all Men are created equal, that they are endowed by their Creator with certain unalienable Rights, that among these are Life, Liberty, and the Pursuit of Happiness—That to secure these Rights, Governments are instituted among Men, deriving their just Powers from the Consent of the Governed.[47]

In this succinct passage, the world is put on notice. The government of the soon-to-be-named United States of America will be established by the people and for the people. Its constitution will seek to secure the inalienable rights of life, liberty, and opportunity so that each individual may pursue happiness. Even today, we still enjoy defining ourselves by reference to these aspirations.

And yet the Declaration of Independence does not have the force of positive law. It is typically read as a document whose chief concern is cataloging the failures of King George III—failures so outrageous that they warranted revolution.[48] Though a part of our history, it is not a part of our law because it declares only our separation from Britain and not yet our constitution.[49] To constitute a nation, the story goes, a social contract is required. Perhaps this is true, but I want to stress another observation that is often ignored. We should not overlook the fact that the Declaration also includes a vision of what a postrevolutionary America should look like. The Declaration does more than list causes for separation from Britain; it sets down conditions for just government—constitutional conditions in the unusual sense of conditions upon a constitution.

There are two conditions. The first is a legitimacy condition with regard to the source of authority: It says that legitimate government authority is democratic, that it is derived from the individuals who will be governed. The second condition is teleological; it sets forth the ends of government: to secure the inalienable rights of individuals, specifically rights to life, liberty, and the pursuit of happiness. A just government governs in virtue of the consent of the governed. A good government fosters conditions under which individuals will be free (i.e., capable of choosing for themselves) and under which individuals can pursue happiness.[50]

Many commentators see this first condition as a commitment to limited government.[51] By recognizing that the state derives its power from the people and that the people in fact only conferred limited powers upon the government, they claim that individuals retain a sphere into which the government may not intrude.[52] The argument that democratic government should derive its authority by consent of the governed is persuasive, but focusing on it often engenders a confusion that makes it more difficult to reconsider our present views on individualism. The argument assumes that government may exist to protect individuals from the perils of a state of nature but claims that respect for individual liberty requires government to do nothing beyond this. Rather, it is assumed we would naturally arrive at the conditions of a satisfying individualism—in which independent individuals can develop to their full potential—but for illegitimate intrusion of government.[53] A rock thrown up will, by force of gravity, be drawn to its natural resting place on the earth as long as one does not interfere by catching it. So too, individuals will flourish in their natural state if government does not intrude. Thus, by scrupulously observing the boundaries of its legitimate power, the government provides the necessary conditions to realize the teleological goals of individual liberty and pursuit of happiness.

Unfortunately, this theory for promoting individualism goes badly awry in practice. If government does not intrude into the inner city beyond providing minimal health and safety services, this is no guarantee that individuals who inhabit the inner city are thereby made free. To be free, in the context of present society, means to be able to employ one's creative powers to shape one's world. Individualism, as Emerson recognized, is not a default condition but something to be continually achieved. Emerson prized the ability of individuals to adapt to circumstances and transform them. He saw in such transformation the amazing power of what he called "mind"—what we might understand as the creative potentiality of individuals.

> Everything is pusher or pushed; and matter and mind are in perpetual tilt and balance, so. While the man is weak, the earth takes up him. He plants his brain, and affections. By and by he will take up the earth, and have his gardens and vineyards in the beautiful order and productiveness of his thought. Every solid in the universe is ready to become fluid on the approach of the mind, and the power to flux it is the measure of the mind.[54]

In Emerson's America, a commitment to individualism required helping individuals develop the power to flux the universe, to engage in a transformative relation with the universe. In the context he describes, this requires learning how to engage nature through such activities as gardening and agriculture. In the context of our present age, there is not only a question about the individual's relation to nature but to society as well. How can we empower individuals to actively participate in construction of shared social structures?[55]

What individuals need to develop and grow will change with time and circumstances. Individualism is not about achieving an end state but about participating in a continuing process of self-realization in both senses: a self is being realized and a self is doing the realizing.[56] To further individualism, therefore, is to provide individuals the means to undertake this struggle in the context of their present lives and the obstacles they face. John Dewey emphasizes that the promotion of individualism requires not only rethinking policy in order to protect existing and compelling forms of individualism, but also recognizing that commitment to individualism demands a thorough rethinking of individualism itself in light of changing circumstances.

> Such thinking [assuming that instituting large economic policy changes will simply preserve the traditional forms of individualism] treats individualism as if it were something static, having a uniform content. It ignores the fact that the mental and moral structure of individuals, the pattern of their desires and purposes, change with every great change in social constitution. Individuals, who are not bound together in associations, whether domestic, economic, religious, political, artistic or educational, are monstrosities. It is absurd to suppose that the ties, which hold them together, are merely external and do not react into mentality and character, producing the framework of personal disposition.[57]

Two insights emerge from this examination of individualism. First, the concept must be understood as a social project; second, the meaning of individual empowerment will vary with social circumstance.

At first blush, the proposition that individualism is a social project is paradoxical.[58] Is not the whole point of individualism to privilege the individual, not social agency? How does one protect the individual by placing the fate of the individual in society's hands? Will not concerns for social welfare simply run roughshod over the interests of individuals? Such questions seem vexing until it is realized that concerns for social welfare already sanction disregard for individuals. The fate of individuals already is entwined with our social vision. The question is not whether this should be so, but how this fact will be addressed.

The present form of entanglement is not working out well for individuals. It dictates separating the public interest of society from the private interest of individuals and weighing the two. For example, public interest is served by maintaining a pool of unemployed workers for industry. Individuals' misery constituted by unemployment is not a substantial factor in the equation.[59] Public interest is served by maintaining order in schools, but there is no corresponding call for this order to be reconciled with the needs of the students. The individual needs something more on her side of the scale, but the present separation between public and private interests prevents her from finding what she needs because what she needs is public recognition that individualism is not only in the public interest, but also part and parcel of the very purpose driving social organization.

Communitarians take the opposite approach. They insist that what is most needed is for the individual to cease relying on a selfish conception of rights and become more civic-minded.

> Our stark, simple rights dialect puts a damper on the processes of public justification, communication, and deliberation upon which the continuing vitality of a democratic regime depends. It contributes to the erosion of the habits, practices, and attitudes of respect for others that are the ultimate and surest guarantors of human rights. . . . Our rights-laden public discourse easily accommodates the economic, the immediate, and the personal dimensions of a problem, while it regularly neglects the moral, the long-term, and the social implications.[60]

Glendon's analysis is perceptive if restricted to a select and suspect class of individual rights bearers, namely corporations who use vast wealth toward socially destructive ends. But as an observation covering the class of individuals in general, I think it is woefully inadequate. As individuals participate more and more in managerial structures, in the roles of students and workers, the strong rights vocabulary has less and less application.[61] In the context of schools, the cases discussed above represent a growing trend toward heeding concerns of administration while ignoring claims of individuals. The problem is less a lack of civic-mindedness among individuals and more a failure of different types of institutions to respect individuals.

Consider *Olesen*: The issue is not simply whether the pain a student endures when punished for wearing an earring is outweighed by the people's interest in safety, but whether the people's responsibility for the promotion of individual development is at odds with these laws. Do I sound like a communitarian on these issues? Yes and no. Yes, communitarians are right that we must undermine the opposition inherent in the traditional application of the public/private dichotomy, but not in the manner they suppose. Glendon's analysis implies that individuals should subordinate their desires for self-expression and self-gratification and recover a commitment to self-discipline and self-reliance.[62] But here I part company with communitarians because it is a mistake to imagine these virtues at odds in this way. Self-reliance is a form of self-expression, not its opposite. It is a means to achieving one's unique self-relation to the world. Facilitating this achievement, Emerson believed, was the central mission of each age.

> Our age is retrospective. It builds the sepulchres of the fathers. It writes biographies, histories, and criticism. The foregoing generations beheld God and nature face to face; we, through their eyes. Why should not we also enjoy an original relation to the universe? Why should not we have a poetry and philosophy of insight and not of tradition, and a religion by revelation to us, and not the history of theirs?[63]

Rather than praising the virtues of self-disciplined individuals who subordinate their desires to the public good, we ought to remind the public, following Brandeis and Emerson, that America's highest obligation has always been the development of individuals. Accordingly, our responsibility is to create conditions under which individuals can construct for themselves an original relation to the universe, conditions that are appropriate to the times we live in. This requires protecting individuals in the choices they make for themselves: sexual orientation, political affiliation, their dress. If we look at *Fraser, Olesen,* and perhaps Wiser as signposts marking the way to the future, it is a future where community is defined not by tendencies toward inhibiting tolerance for individuals but, rather, tendencies toward subordination of the individual to the managerial process. Contrary to the communitarian way of thinking, such a future will require greater attention to individual rights—not less.

Taking a pragmatic approach to rights, and ultimately to law, can help address these concerns. Pragmatic attention to context and purpose in evaluating the meaning of rights helps focus the attention of judges and others upon the most significant issues germane to rethinking rights for the present. Unlike views that tie the meaning of right to the intentions of political founders whose lives were quite remote from the present, pragmatism insists that the meaning of rights, such as the right to freedom of expression, can be discovered only through attention to the variety of contexts in which those rights are exercised. In a discussion of genetic method, Dewey describes the merits of a pragmatic approach, which pays particular attention to the context in which intuitions originate. The analysis is equally helpful in considering the development and future of rights.

> The point of the genetic method is then that it shows relationships, and thereby at once guarantees and defines meaning. We must take the history of any intuition or attitude of moral consciousness in both directions: *both ex parte ante and ex parte post*. We must consider it with reference to the antecedents which evoked it, and with reference to its later career and fate. It arises in a certain context, and as a reaction to certain circumstances; it has a subsequent history which can be traced. It maintains and reinforces certain conditions, and modifies others. It becomes a stimulus which provokes new modes of action. Now when we see how and why the belief came about, and also know what else came about because of it, we have a hold upon the worth of the belief which is entirely wanting when we set it up as an isolated intuition.[64]

Taking Dewey's approach in thinking about rights yields interesting results. First, historically understood, rights are an attempt to secure economic and political self-determination for those laboring under feudalism.[65] At their origin, therefore, "rights" are creatures of context. Second, the meaning of a right changes as it is extended into new contexts. This is why questions about the nature of cyberspace are so pressing. Is posting a political edict in a cyberspace chat room the equivalent of leafleting on the town square or soliciting in an airport? Until we decide on the appropriate analogical extension, the present meaning of the right is indeterminate.

Pragmatists also insist that when a judge rethinks the meaning of a right for the present, she should do so with an eye toward future contexts. She must ask what form protections against interference with freedom of expression should take in order to protect individuals in the future that appears most likely. This approach to rights and adjudication is promising, but if Ronald Dworkin is correct, then this pragmatic approach is illegitimate because it misunderstands the nature of rights.[66]

> Pragmatism does not rule out any theory about what makes a community better. But it does not take legal rights seriously. It rejects what other conceptions of law accept: that people can have distinctly

legal rights as trumps over what would otherwise be the best future properly understood. According to pragmatism what we call legal rights are only the servants of the best future: they are instruments we construct for that purpose and have no independent force or ground.[67]

Dworkin argues that individuals possess rights that function as trumps against pursuit of the collective goals of society. These rights are based on an idea of political equality that supposes minorities in a political community are entitled to concern and respect equal to that given to the majority. Dworkin's account of rights has affinities with Kant's injunction that we should treat individuals as ends in themselves, not simply as means to further ends.[68]

Pragmatism, in Dworkin's view, resists endorsing the majority conception of community, or any particular conception for that matter, but it does not "take legal rights seriously." At most, pragmatism recognizes "as-if rights," viz., it "pretends" that people have rights because such pretense aids in the construction of a better future. But why does Dworkin call such rights "as-if"? Presumably, for pragmatists, what it means for something to be a legal right is for it to have certain functions in the development of a better community. William James' formulation of pragmatism underscores the importance of this appeal to function and experience:

> Pragmatism, on the other hand, asks its usual question. "Grant an idea or belief to be true," it says, "what concrete difference will its being true make in anyone's actual life? How will truth be realized? What experiences will be different from those which would obtain if the belief were false? What, in short, is the truth's cash-value in experiential terms?[69]

How would an individual's pragmatic "as-if" rights differ from Dworkin's very serious legal rights in experience? To answer this question, we must compare the kind of rights generated in connection with a pragmatic account of a better future with the kind of rights embedded in Dworkin's account of political equality. Thus we return to the question we posed earlier: What do pragmatists think is best or, properly understood, better for the future?

They do not think it is best to impose any one conception of the "best community." In practice, therefore, the best community for pragmatists is one that allows for a multiplicity of visions of the best community. It is one that values participation of individuals in its very formation—"[e]quality and freedom expressed not merely externally and politically, but through personal participation in the development of shared culture."[70]

For Dewey, this vision of the better community can be summed up by the name "democracy." It is captured in "Jefferson's formulation," which is "moral through and through: in its foundations, its method, its ends. The heart of [Jefferson's] faith is expressed in his words 'Nothing is unchangeable but inherent and inalienable rights of man.'"[71] These "inalienable" rights, and the moral ideals that spawned them, are "not located in the clouds but are backed by something deep and indestructible in the needs and demands of humankind."[72] To recognize individual rights in this sense is to facilitate ever-greater self-expression and self-actualization of individuals; this is the pragmatic vision of a better future. It has important affinities with Dworkin's concept of political equality inasmuch as treating people with equal concern and respect involves securing for them the conditions necessary for self-expression and self-actualization—in short, for individual growth. Dewey sums up the responsibilities of government and social institutions that flow from his conception of democracy/community:

> Government, business, art, religion, all social institutions have a meaning, a purpose. That purpose is to set free and to develop the capacities of human individuals without respect to race, sex, class or economic status. And this is all one with saying that the test of their value is the extent to which they educate every individual into the full stature of his possibility.[73]

On this account, the goal of a better community and the development of the potentialities of its members are not competing goals, but the same one. Dworkin's view of rights as individual trumps against an otherwise "best future" is incompatible with Dewey's pragmatic vision. Pragmatism rejects any future as best that deprives individual(s) of active participation in the construction and formulation of that future. This does not mean that it is never appropriate to understand rights as trumps. Judges may frequently have occasion to treat rights as individual trumps in order to prohibit the majority imposition of a tyrannical "best future." Yet rights must function as more than trumps for pragmatists. They are a part of the visions of better communities in a participatory democracy. In contradistinction, the notion of collective goals over and against individual goals is an impediment to grasping the full contextual surroundings of the problem of freedom, as well as a roadblock to the construction of more inclusive visions of a better future.

> Estimate of the value of any proposed policy is held back by taking the problem as if it were one of individual "forces" on one side and of social forces on the other, the nature of the forces being known in advance. We must start from another set of premises if we are to put the problem of freedom in the context where it belongs.
>
> The questions . . . demand discussion of cultural conditions, conditions of science, art, morals, religion, education, and industry, so as to discover which of them in actuality promote and which retard the development of the native constituents of human nature. If we want individuals to be free we must see to it that suitable conditions exist—a truism which at least indicates the direction in which to look and move.[74]

These suitable conditions for self-actualization are not indefinitely fixed and stable but change over time, as does the makeup of individuals. For example, growth and free expression were served at one time by a conception of negative freedom (i.e., freedom *from* constraints). Individualism flourished under a scheme of laissez-faire economics, which allowed individual development in an unregulated market of exchange. Such exchange, at that time, granted the participants equality of opportunity. Indeed, this system of exchange and political organization devoid of the leadership of a divinely designated king was, at the time Locke wrote, an extremely radical proposal.

Today, the freedom necessary for the expression of individualism is positive (i.e., freedom *to*). Equality of opportunity requires regulation of economic conditions to make free choice possible.[75] Unfortunately, there is often a lag between changes in technology and the consonant evolution of ideas and desires.[76] Ideas that were originally liberating, such as Locke's conception of freedom, applied unreflectively to the changed conditions of modern life, produce non-freedom for large segments of the population. For example, look at the unequal opportunity for active participation and self-direction in modern economic markets afforded to those who receive substandard education in the ghettos of large cities. It is insignificant with respect to "free choice" that the government generally does not interfere with these individuals' career selection since their job opportunities have already been substantially narrowed by the low quality of their education.

Thus, the role of a pragmatic intelligence, particularly in judicial decisionmaking, is the continuing critical examination, interpretation, and practical application of our (constitutional) values in conjunction with the changing conditions of experience. Pragmatic jurisprudence attempts to guide the evolution of legal institutions to better serve individual growth, as well as form a larger, more integrated view of legal matters with the broader array of general social concerns.

> Moreover, when it is systematically acknowledged in practice that social facts are going concerns and that all legal matters have their place within these ongoing concerns, there will be a much stronger likelihood than at present that new knowledge will be acquired of a kind which can be brought to bear upon the never-ending process of improving standards of judgment.[77]

Dworkin claims, however, that in their attempt to develop a better future, pragmatists do not take rights seriously, but only instrumentally.

> According to pragmatism what we call legal rights are *only* the servants of the best future: they are instruments we construct for that purpose and have no independent force or ground.[78]

He is correct that, for pragmatists, rights are not independent except in their relation to a better future, but he is wrong to suggest that rights are therefore *only* instrumentally valuable (as opposed to intrinsically valuable). The guarantees of constitutional rights, chief among them the right to free expression, are ends which must always be understood in their relation to other ends and the ever-evolving needs of individuals. Dworkin seems to think this requirement denigrates the status of rights to mere "servants of the best future." This is misleading. For pragmatists, rights do not merely serve a vision of a better future; they are a part of any such future. Moreover, given the pragmatic theory of valuation, any vision of a better future (not "best future") is itself not an isolated ultimate end but an end that is also a means toward further ends. Hence, the vision is itself, in some sense, a servant of still other visions—but that is not to say it, or the action required to bring it about, is without value. As Dewey points out, use of pragmatic intelligence is an end as well as a means, even though it is most definitely instrumental.

> Intelligence is, indeed, instrumental *through* action to the determination of the qualities of future experience. But the very fact that the concern of intelligence is with the future, with the as-yet-unrealized (and with the given and the established only as conditions of the realization of possibilities), makes the action in which it takes effect generous and liberal; free of spirit. Just that action which extends and approves intelligence has an intrinsic value of its own in being instrumental:—the intrinsic value of being informed with intelligence in behalf of the enrichment of life.[79]

Dworkin is wrong to write off pragmatic rights as fake or merely "as-if." For pragmatists, the realness of rights is a function of trying to understand rights in the context in which they emerge while also considering the impact of our present understanding on the way we will live together in the future.

TWO

Taking Rights and Pragmatism Seriously

Dworkin's resistance to pragmatism is not limited to pragmatic accounts of rights. More generally, he believes that pragmatism cannot
provide a coherent answer to the question, "What is law?" His attack
on the pragmatist theory of jurisprudence is built around his claim
that a pragmatic judge would be indifferent to past political decisions
of the courts or legislature. In addition, Dworkin throws in charges of
subjectivism, deceptive manipulation of precedent, and a general lack
of systemization. These attacks are ill-founded. The purpose of this
chapter is not only to show the error of Dworkin's ways, but also to
deepen our appreciation for all that pragmatism has to offer our understanding of the role of law in social life, particularly with reference
to securing conditions for the flourishing of individuals.

Just who counts as a pragmatist for Dworkin is difficult to ascertain. He cites none by name, and although initially aligning pragmatism with legal realism, he distinguishes the former from the latter
by its interpretive rather than semantic attitude.[1] This general failure
of identification is disturbing, particularly in association with the me-

diocre version of pragmatism Dworkin proffers. His recognition that "perhaps no legal philosopher would defend"[2] his formulation of pragmatism serves only to heighten suspicion that one is witnessing the construction of a straw man. In any case, I accept the challenge to pragmatism on behalf of the version developed by John Dewey.[3] As I will show, Dewey not only eludes Dworkin's criticisms but also enables us to better understand Dworkin's own achievements.

With reference to pragmatism, Dworkin writes:

> The pragmatist takes a skeptical attitude toward the assumption we are assuming is embodied in the concept of law: he denies that past political decisions in themselves provide any justification for either using or withholding the state's coercive power. He finds the necessary justification for coercion in the justice or efficiency or some other contemporary virtue of the coercive decision itself, as and when it is made by judges and adds that consistency with any past legislative or judicial decision does not in principle contribute to the justice or virtue of any present one. If judges are guided by this advice, he believes, then unless they make great mistakes, the coercion they direct will make the community's future brighter, liberated from the dead hand of the past and the fetish of consistency for its own sake.
>
> Of course, [pragmatist] judges will disagree about which rule, laid down in which circumstances, would in fact be best for the future without concern for the past.[4]

The most basic flaw Dworkin locates in a pragmatist theory of law is its refusal to value consistency with past decisions *in principle*. I believe he is right that pragmatists do not value consistency for its own sake but wrong to consider this a flaw. Pragmatists, as I will show, value consistency as a means to further ends. It does not follow from this assessment that pragmatists would eschew historical consistency altogether, nor would such an understanding even seem possible to one acquainted with pragmatic method.

Dworkin mysteriously infers from his claim that pragmatism would not value consistency for its own sake the further claim that pragmatism's zealous quest for what is "best for the future" is unconcerned with the past. This conclusion rests on the assumption that pragmatism's conception of what is "best for the future" bears no important relation to the past either in its development of future goals or in its methodological pursuit of such goals. It ascribes to pragmatism a will toward a brighter, quasi-utopian future, created by the liberation of reason from the weight of historical experience in custom and tradition. It is reminiscent of the numerous commentators who quote Emerson, a forerunner of pragmatism, as saying, "consistency is the hobgoblin of little minds."[5] The implication is that not only does Emerson reject consistency as good in itself, but he also suggests consistency is bad in itself. It is this latter attitude that Dworkin seems to be implicitly urging in his reading of pragmatism. To accept this attitude is to miss as much in a pragmatic reading of law as was missed in the above quotation of Emerson's accurately rendered: "A *foolish* consistency is the hobgoblin of little minds."[6]

To evaluate Dworkin's criticism, we need to cultivate an understanding of what it would mean for a pragmatist to make his decisions based on a conception of what is "best for the future." It is certainly true that pragmatism is forward-looking, as Dworkin suggests. It recognizes that social conditions are continually changing and that "the important question is whether intelligence, whether observation and reflection, intervenes and becomes a directive factor in the transition."[7] The projected goals of this guided evolution, however, do not arise outside of our history but within it. They arise in the conditions of historical experience and function as a response to that experience.

> To be good is to be better than; and there can be no better except where there is shock and discord combined with enough assured order to make attainment of harmony possible. . . . Water that slakes thirst, or a conclusion that solves a problem have ideal character as long as thirst or problem persists in a way which qualifies the result. But water that is not a satisfaction of need has no more ideal quality than water running through pipes into a reservoir; a solution ceases to be a solution and becomes a bare incident of existence when its antecedent generating conditions of doubt, ambiguity and search are lost from its context.[8]

The function of pragmatic philosophical thought, stated negatively, is criticism—the amelioration of the problems encountered in lived experience. Dewey often refers to such philosophical thought as "intelligence" or "criticism" to avoid the misreading that he is talking about a narrow group of so-called "philosophical" problems. His project is broader in scope than traditional "philosophical" pursuits: It rejects the separation of academic disciplines, such as "anthropology, history, sociology, morals, economics, political science,"[9] etc., as anathemas to the development of social knowledge. This fracturing of thought among disciplines exacerbates the academic tendency to rip problems out of their original context and meaning. It exports them to the insulated realms of academic scrutiny where they are transformed from problems of lived experience to problems of "philosophy." The appropriate context for the problems of lived experience is the larger social and cultural context in which they arise.

> The state of culture is a state of interaction of many factors, the chief of which are law and politics, industry and commerce, science and technology, the arts of expression and communication, and of morals, or the values men prize and the ways in which they evaluate them; and finally . . . their social philosophy.[10]

Stated positively, the function of "intelligence" is to actively guide the development of community and individual as an interrelated whole. The goal of this guidance is the establishment of conditions for self-actualization and self-fulfillment of individual potentialities in and with the larger community.

> The problem of constructing a new individuality consonant with the objective conditions under which we live is the deepest problem of our times. . . . The first step in further definition of this problem is realization of the collective age which we have already entered. When that is apprehended, the issue will define itself as utilization of the realities of a corporate civilization to validate and embody the distinctive moral element in the American version of individualism: Equality and freedom expressed not merely externally and politically but through personal participation in the development of a shared culture.[11]

Given this account of pragmatism, it is inconceivable that pragmatists would deal with what "would in fact be best for the future without concern for the past."[12] The standard by which they assess what is best for the future is in relation to the problems of the present arrived at through the past. Dworkin's use of the phrase "best for the future" is, in part, responsible for painting a misleading picture of the pragmatic project. As noted above, the pragmatic criterion of good is not "best," but "better than." The term "best" underplays the importance of the relation between future and past. It overemphasizes the notion of teleological progression toward some separate future ideal. Pragmatism voices ideals but not as "hard and rigid"[13] goals separate from both the context in which they arise and the process by which they are pursued. On the contrary, such ideals of direction for human action, posited from a particular historical standpoint, are reshaped as the conditions from which they were originally articulated are transformed. Pragmatists, far from being unconcerned with the past, must be particularly sensitive to it. It is there that the desires that have bred their conception of a brighter future and the instruments for its achievement can be found.

> The essential continuity of history is doubly guaranteed. Not only are personal desire and belief functions of habit and custom, but the objective conditions which provide the resources and tools of action, together with its limitations, obstructions and traps are precipitates of the past, perpetuating, willy-nilly, its hold and power. The creation of a tabula rasa in order to permit the creation of a new order is so impossible as to set at naught both the hope of buoyant revolutionaries and the timidity of scared conservatives.[14]

It is obvious that pragmatism's account of what is "best for the future" is intimately tied up with its concern for the past and present. However, thus far I have discussed only pragmatism's general concern with the past, which, although implicated in Dworkin's attack, is not the focal point. The crux of Dworkin's attack is the pragmatist's general disrespect for past "legislative and judicial" decisions.

> The pragmatist thinks judges should always do the best they can for the future, in the circumstances, unchecked by any need to respect or secure consistency in principle with what other officials have done or will do.[15]

> [The pragmatist] rejects, it is true, the very idea of consistency in principle as important for its own sake.[16]

Dworkin's claims are laden with misleading implications. Presumably when Dworkin claims that the pragmatist does not value consistency "in principle" or "for its own sake," he means that the pragmatist does not think consistency is valuable except in relation to some other values (i.e., consistency is not an end in itself). This is quite correct, but it is impossible to understand why pragmatists hold this view without connecting it up to a pragmatic theory of valuation. To facilitate such understanding, I will develop a brief account of Dewey's theory of valuation.

If moral claims about what is "best for the future" are claims of the form "X is good, X is valuable, or X is right," then these claims can be rationally justified by appeal to how they are situated amongst other moral ends. Dewey claims that propositions about valuations are factual propositions that can be empirically tested. These propositions are derived from valuations that are composed of the activities of "prizing" and "appraising." To prize something is to claim that it will satisfy certain desire(s). To appraise something is to assign it value with respect to other ends; thus, appraising is always teleological. All actions are assessed with an end-in-view, and ends realized are means to other ends-in-view.

Desiring is itself an act of bringing something into existence. Desires are responses to dissatisfaction—as one experiences a gap between the actual conditions of the present and the possibility of improving those conditions, desires are born. They arise out of experienced needs that are unfulfilled at present but are capable of fulfillment. They are distinct from mere wishes because they involve undertaking actions designed to ameliorate these experienced needs, whereas wishes are the expression of various needs devoid of corresponding action to achieve their fulfillment. Desiring is an impetus to further action, prized with respect to some valued (appraised) end; that valued end is, in turn, valued with respect to some other end, and so on, ad infinitum.

Means and ends describe action in an operational, not intrinsic, sense. The distinction between "means" and "ends" is not a distinction of kind but merely of temporal/historical relation. The ends desired are continually transformed by the process of valuation itself. Even as an end-in-view is realized, the new conditions brought about by its realization lead to the creation of new desires. In this way, value propositions become the subject matter of further valuations. Thus, the process of valuation is ongoing. Initially, I am sick and experience the need to become well, which in turn is desired in order that I may exercise, which is desired so that I may accomplish something else, etc. When health is restored, this whole rationalization evolves in light of the new needs this change has brought about. Valuation does not terminate with the achievement of an end in itself because the achievement of any particular end is met with the revelation of still more ends-in-view. All ends are also ends-in-view.

The course of action undertaken to satisfy desires is justified to the extent that it does, in fact, satisfy the desire that was its original motivation without giving rise to an even more unsatisfying experience, or to the extent that it undermines the perceived import of satisfying the original desire at all. Hence, we can critically assess our original hypothesis that "X is the best for the future" by its consequences with respect to how well it resolves or dissolves the problems of the original experience in which it arose.

Thus when Dworkin claims that the pragmatist does not value consistency as an end in itself, he is right. This does not mean that the pragmatist does not value consistency for other reasons in its relation to other values. So it is the case that

> The pragmatist thinks judges should always do the best they can for the future, in the circumstances, unchecked by any need to respect or secure consistency *in principle* with what other officials have done or will do.[17]

But it is not the case that

> The pragmatist thinks judges should always do the best they can for the future, in the circumstances, unchecked by *any* need to respect or secure consistency with what other officials have done or will do.

There are a number of reasons pragmatists are likely to respect what other officials have done and be concerned with what they will do. They might argue that consistency in legal decisions is valuable because it aids individuals in anticipating and guiding their behavior according to legal precepts while avoiding costly litigation. Or they could maintain that consistency is valuable because it cultivates a sense of fairness in the application of the law. Fairness and predictability are not, on this model, ends in themselves only but ends that are also means toward further ends.

Pragmatism views knowledge as a cumulative product of collective experience; ignoring the previous valuations of other judges would be tantamount to proceeding irrationally. Dworkin's account makes it sound as if the pragmatist is liable to make radical breaks with past judicial and legislative valuations at any moment. Not only does this account fail to recognize the "essential continuity of history,"[18] but it also fails to grasp that pragmatic changes are not "breaks" with past valuations so much as they are evolutionary extensions of these valuations.

> These considerations lead to the central question: What are the conditions that have to be met so that knowledge of the past and existing valuations becomes an instrumentality of valuation in formation of new desires and interests—of desires and interests that the test of experience show to be best worth fostering? . . .
>
> The answer is that improved valuation must grow out of existing valuations, subjected to critical methods of investigation that bring them into systematic relations with one another.[19]

The pragmatist does not even know how to make sense of consistency as an end in itself. "Consistency" is a relational term that describes a relationship between valuations. The case for making present decisions consistent with past decisions depends on two things: First, the degree of similarity between the conditions of experience that motivated the past decision and the conditions that are motivating the present decision; second, the consequences of the past decision with respect to the problem it attempted to solve.

Dworkin describes the pragmatic jurist's use of precedent as the "strategic" use of a "noble-lie" in order to bring about his vision of the best future.[20] Although he admits that pragmatism will make some use of the doctrine of precedent in clear cases so that "people can plan their affairs with more confidence,"[21] he concludes that for pragmatists,

> This justification for respecting past precedent does not hold when the scope of a past decision is unclear and controversial. So a pragmatist has no direct reason to strain to discover the "true" ground of that decision by attempting to read the minds of the judges who decided it or by any other process of divination. Nor does he feel compelled to decide later cases "by analogy" to earlier ones, at least when there is room for disagreement about whether a later case is really like or unlike them.[22]

Again, what Dworkin is saying is full of misleading suggestions, and it is simply amazing that he thinks this account undercuts the pragmatist's position. Dworkin assumes that the pragmatist simply cannot wait to free himself from the obligation of following precedent so that he can "decide as he thinks best, on a fresh slate."[23] This misses the pragmatic point. Although pragmatists are interested in developing precedent to help people plan, their primary interest is to see that legal decisions function as effective solutions to the host of problems that gave rise to them (including, of course, the need for predictability). Their interest in analogies amongst cases is by no means an artificial aspect of their deliberation toward this end, but an integral step in any such valuation. They rely heavily on the consequences of past decisions to form their hypotheses concerning the likely consequences of their present decision, taking into account as best they can the different conditions of experience that distinguish these cases.

Admittedly, pragmatists will not feel "compelled to decide later cases by analogy to earlier ones" when "the scope of a past decision is unclear and controversial." But if Dworkin is suggesting that judges should feel compelled to so decide, how they would do so, given the "unclear" conditions posited by Dworkin's description, is no small mystery. Furthermore, while I doubt pragmatists will "strain to discover the 'true' ground of that decision by attempting to read the minds of the judges who decided it," they will probably "strain" to elicit whatever connections between past cases and the present case could better inform their valuation. Pragmatic decisions are not *tabula rasa* affairs, but rather grow out of criticism of existing decisions. Having elicited these connections, pragmatists would then decide whether making a similar decision would be desirable.

It is important to note that the issue of whether a present case shares relevant legal characteristics with a past case is extremely complex. To claim that a present case should be decided like a past case, one must establish the prior claim that the present case is, in terms of legal aspect, similar to the past case. It is of little help in clarifying the decisions of pragmatic judges (or the decisions of any judge) to claim that they do not decide present cases with respect to past cases unless it is also established that the present cases so named are, in fact, similar to the past cases. This is, of course, precisely what is at issue. Dworkin never establishes a critical framework from which to evaluate the criteria of similarity employed by pragmatic judges. Instead, he blindly asserts that pragmatists not only fail to value consistency in principle, but also seemingly value inconsistency or flexibility in principle.

> Imagine a pragmatist judge deciding McLoughlin. He sets aside the question whether there is any important difference between the case of a mother who suffers emotional injury watching her child hit by a car and a mother who suffers the same sort of injury seeing her child bloody in a hospital. He insists that these cases be divorced. . . . Linking the two cases does not promote planning, since the link is in any case controversial, and flexibility is improved by separating them.[24]

Dworkin gives us absolutely no reason why the pragmatist judge would set aside the question of "whether there is any important difference of principle" between these two cases. Indeed, on the pragmatic model of valuation I have set forth, such considerations would be essential to the pragmatist in formulating his decisions. Dworkin contends that the pragmatist is predisposed toward separating cases to allow for "flexibility." Yet if pragmatists are so inclined, it must certainly not be explained by unreflective adherence to flexibility for its own sake, for such would be an extreme departure from a pragmatic theory of valuation. If consistency is not, in principle, valuable to the pragmatist, it is difficult to see why flexibility would be.

Dworkin's insistence that pragmatists have strong desires for flexibility is the result of his mistaken belief that pragmatists feel trapped by precedent. They do not. They will apply precedent to cases that, in their judgment, are relevantly similar to past cases, and they will not apply precedent to cases that are not.[25] Perhaps they will find more differences between two cases than Dworkin would. If so, it remains to be argued whose understanding of the relation between the two cases is better. Pragmatism is anything but hostile, in principle, to studying the relations between present and previous decisions. After all, only through such comparisons can present decisions be improved.

> Such an impression [that improved valuations cannot grow out of existing, generally defective ones] arises only because of failure to consider how they actually may be brought into relation with one another, namely, by examination of their respective conditions and consequences. Only by following this path will they be reduced to such homogeneous terms that they are comparable to one another.[26]

As we have seen, the pragmatic conception of law is more respect-
ful of past decisions than Dworkin has imagined. It respects not only
the past decision but the historical context in which that decision was
made. It looks to the accumulated knowledge for guidance in making
present decisions, and it does not fail to note the novel aspects of those
present decisions. Pragmatism does not view any goal as merely an end
in itself. Even desires for individual development and growth are not
correctly described as goods in themselves but, rather, in relation to the
satisfaction of the deeply rooted needs that invoke them. Thus, pragmatism takes legal rights seriously both as means for achieving a better
community (in the sense of being more responsive to the demands of
individuals) as well as ends inasmuch as those rights are themselves
part of that better community.

Ultimately, however, pragmatic goals and visions of a better community are always of a hypothetical form, awaiting judgment according to the consequences they produce in experience. Dworkin asserts
that the model of jurisprudence that best fits and describes the activity
of our courts, and best justifies its history, is the answer to the question:
What is law? A pragmatist judge would not worry primarily about
whether pragmatic jurisprudence fits and describes our political institutions. She would worry, instead, about how such a description
functions as a means to further ends, namely, ameliorating the problems we encounter in that experience we are concerned to describe.
Pragmatism is a method that studies previous decisions and tries to
make better ones. Its acceptance as a theory of jurisprudence should be
based on the success or failure of employing the insights generated
from its method.

> If different contributions to this volume [legal philosophies] repre-
> sent incompatible positions, it is because they express different atti-
> tudes toward practical questions of what should be done and how
> best to do it. At all events, what I myself have to say is put forth in this
> spirit. Fundamentally, a program for action to be tested in action set
> forth, not something that can be judged (beyond assertion of fact
> and matters of logical consistency) on a purely intellectual basis.[27]

I hope I have been successful in establishing, at least theoretically,
the plausibility of both a pragmatic understanding and defense of
rights as well as a more general jurisprudence that is deeply historical

and committed to the forward-looking guidance of social evolution, particularly with regard to the well-being of individuals. Ironically, in theory, such jurisprudence appears strikingly similar to Dworkin's law as integrity. In order to explore the similarity, we must know not only how Dworkin's judge decides various cases, but also why. This is almost impossible to determine from Dworkin's examples. Dworkin employs his legal superhero Hercules, who possesses "superhuman intellectual power and patience"[28] and can take into account all the relevant decisions of political institutions. But when he is finished investigating particular cases, the most important aspects of the decisions in those cases are often posited on the authority of Hercules rather than developed by argument.

It is worth noting that the usefulness of Hercules, the super jurist as a heuristic device for constructing a coherent account of law, is problematic. It is similar in tone to Peirce's conception of truth as the conclusion that a community of scientific investigators, investigating infinitely, would arrive at. But there is an important difference: Peirce never attempts to tell us what those investigators would decide, but Dworkin does tell us what Hercules decides. In light of this, it does not seem unreasonable to expect Dworkin to supply a comprehensive account of Hercules' reasons in particular cases rather than deferring to his built-in authority.

To take a typical example, in *Brown* Hercules overrules the precedent *Plessy* without hesitation, according to Dworkin.[29] This is somewhat shocking given the importance Dworkin attributes to maintaining consistency in principle. The explanation of this event is as follows:

> Perhaps this theory [of racial equality] would have been adequate under tests of fairness and fit at sometime in our history; perhaps it would have been adequate when *Plessy* was decided. It is not adequate now, nor was it in 1954 when Hercules had to decide *Brown*. It gains little support from the ideals of political fairness. The American people would almost unanimously have rejected it, even in 1954, as not faithful to their convictions about racial justice.[30]

Unfortunately, Dworkin does not tell us why this theory is inadequate, nor does he describe any of the changes in experience that led to its inadequacy. Finally, it is unclear what the import of his last reference to the convictions of the American public is. It would appear that this provides *de facto* support for his claim that the first theory of racial equality, suspect classification, was inadequate for critically assessing *Brown*. But why should we insist that constitutional decision criteria be in accord with the convictions of the general populace? After all, if Dewey is right that there is a lag between changes in the conditions of experience and changes in the ideals and valuations of individuals to correspond with that experience, then it is likely that good selection criteria that correct this imbalance will appear radical. It is highly unlikely that such criteria will be faithful to popular convictions; otherwise, there would be no imbalance between existing conditions and values.

In any case, it is difficult, if not impossible, to understand why Hercules arrives at the decision to reject *Plessy*. Clearly, Dworkin does view this as an inconsistent decision that fails to respect past decisions:

> [Hercules] was untroubled about overruling *Plessy* in deciding *Brown*; but this is not the whole story because his attitude toward precedents would be more respectful when he was asked to restrict the constitutional rights they had enforced than when he was asked to reaffirm their denials of such rights.[31]

Whatever justification Hercules ends up providing for his break with precedent, it will most likely take the form of a claim that the achievement of some other goal outweighed the concern with consistency. But why is this other goal valuable? Is it also valued in principle, and under what circumstances should we break with it? The best answers here will be pragmatic. Unless we are to subscribe to a form of natural law, we will always be considering consequences relative to ends we esteem.

Dworkin's dominant criticism of the pragmatic judge is that such a judge would be all too willing to ignore precedent for the sake of imposing a ruling that would yield the best future. Indeed, on Dworkin's dim assessment, pragmatists lack integrity because they don't recognize the need to follow precedent in principle, independent of some extra motivating instrumental need. Of the many problems in Dworkin's reading of pragmatism, two stand out: First, he gives absolutely no reason why a pragmatist judge's vision of a better future would not involve protecting goals such as fairness, stability in the legal system, the promotion of predictability to facilitate planning by legal actors, and a variety of other issues that are effected by recognition of precedent. Of course, this just leads us down the pragmatic road of debating the consequences of particular decisions and the relative merit of the various ends for which those decisions are undertaken. In the end, the debate is not between Dworkin's judge of integrity who values precedent for its own sake and the pragmatist who does not, but between judges who take different positions on the overriding goals of the legal system and/or the methods for realizing those goals in particular cases.

The second, and more significant, oversight in Dworkin's critique of the pragmatic judge is his failure to recognize that for significant proponents of pragmatism, such as James and Dewey, our very access to the values by which we would regulate the outcome of cases to achieve the "best" future is dependent upon historical inquiry. Accordingly, the pragmatic judge is likely to take precedent—understood as past determinations of legal value—very seriously indeed. This is not to say that she will force the present into legal standards of the past,[32] but that she must decide two things: (a) whether the values championed in past legal decisions should still hold sway in light of developing legal norms, and (b) whether realizing those values can be achieved in the same way as in the past.[33] Justice Cardozo captured this pragmatic program in his seminal work on the nature of judicial process:

> The situation would, however, be intolerable if the weekly changes in the composition of the court were accompanied by changes in its rulings. In such circumstances there is nothing to do except to stand by the errors of our brethren of the week before, whether we relish them or not. But I am ready to concede that the rule of adherence to precedent, though it ought not to be abandoned, ought to be in some degree relaxed. I think that when a rule, after it has been duly tested by experience, has been found to be inconsistent with the sense of justice or with the social welfare, there should be less hesitation in frank avowal and full abandonment.[34]

The problem with pragmatism as a guide to jurisprudence is not that it does not take precedent seriously, but rather that it does not take it mechanically in a way that fosters easy or uniform prediction. It is a mystery why this should count against pragmatists in Dworkin's view, especially in considering hard cases as precisely those in which the precedents are either unclear or likely to give rise to substantive injustice. It is true that thinkers often gravitate to the security that simple maxims, such as an injunction to follow precedent, seem to offer. Dewey was well aware of the tendency of thinkers to prize the simple and abstract over the actual and messy. He claimed that philosophers often sought to discover elements that were simple and predictable so that

> the mind can rest trustfully in it, knowing that it has no surprises in store, that it will not spring anything to make trouble, that it will stay put, having no potentialities in reserve.[35]

Cardozo himself admitted that when he first became a judge, he was disheartened to discover how uncertain the law actually was.

> I was troubled in spirit, in my first years upon the bench, to find how trackless was the ocean on which I had embarked. I sought for certainty. I was oppressed and disheartened when I found that the quest for it was futile. I was trying to reach land, the solid land of fixed and settled rules, the paradise of a justice that would declare itself by tokens plainer and more commanding than its pale and glimmering reflections in my own vacillating mind and conscience. I found "with the voyagers in Browning's 'Paracelsus' that the real heaven was always beyond." As the years have gone by, and as I have reflected more and more upon the nature of the judicial process, I have become reconciled to the uncertainty, because I have grown to see that the process in its highest reaches is not discovery, but creation; and that the doubts and misgivings, the hopes and fears, are part of the travail of mind, the pangs of death and the pangs of birth, in which principles that have served their day expire, and new principles are born.[36]

While it would be foolish to deny the existence of these tendencies to exalt the simple, it is equally wrong to let them dominate. Although pragmatism may indeed countenance widening judicial inquiry by considering questions of contemporary social context in such a way that distinctions amongst cases will multiply and the force of *stare decisis* diminish, the central question is one of consequence. Will that make for better or worse law given the needs of the present? This is a difficult question to raise, but the alternative to facing this head-on is not so much to avoid the question as to mask one's engagement with it.

Although Ronald Dworkin has been the leading philosopher of rights in America for the last thirty years, he misunderstands and rejects the theory best able to support rights in the present, namely pragmatism. But in rejecting a pragmatic account of rights on the grounds that pragmatism is insufficiently dedicated to history and principle, he leaves his own theory in limbo, never quite able to explain the normative basis for the rights recognized by his theory of law as integrity once appeal to the pragmatic relevance of history is ruled out of court. The consequence is not simply puzzlement for theory, but problems for practice since the effect of Dworkin's criticism that pragmatists don't care about rights is that pragmatism doesn't get taken seriously as an alternative, more substantial basis for the individual rights position that the communitarians seek to undermine. An unhealthy dichotomy is allowed to emerge wherein one identifies with the communitarian recoil at the way in which rights appear to interfere with the exercise of progressive public reason, or one identifies with the quasi-Kantian aspirations of Dworkin's judge to regulate the excesses of a utilitarian social politics by appeal to rights. A third, more promising pragmatic approach is ignored, one which takes rights seriously not by denying but by embracing communitarian demands to explicitly take up questions of a better American future. It is ignored because Dworkin's claim that pragmatic concern with the best future is incompatible with respect for rights has been taken at face value and has not been subject to the scrutiny it deserves.

THREE

Posner's Unpragmatic Pragmatism

I am not the only one who has sought to extricate pragmatism from Dworkin's charges that it makes a virtue of ignoring history. Richard Posner, who has been developing an account of pragmatism for well over a decade, has also come to pragmatism's defense. Unfortunately, despite Posner's spirited effort, endorsing his affirmative view of pragmatism would probably be worse for pragmatism than allowing Dworkin's characterization to go unchallenged.[1]

Posner's most comprehensive effort to develop his version of pragmatism is in his recent book, titled *Law, Pragmatism and Democracy*.[2] He has two goals in writing this book: to explore the implications of pragmatism in law and to discuss the relationship between legal pragmatism and democracy.[3] The central thrust of pragmatism for Posner is the rejection of "pieties" and "conceptualisms"; "the pragmatist's conception of human nature is unillusioned. Among the conceptualisms rejected are moral, legal, and political theory when offered to guide legal and official decisionmaking."[4]

Although acknowledging roots in a lineage of classical pragmatists and adopting many of the key ideas of these thinkers, Posner breaks ranks, advocating a brand of pragmatism he calls "everyday pragmatism."[5] Posner labels the contemporary philosophical tradition that has grown out of pragmatism as "orthodox" and concludes that "orthodox pragmatism has little to contribute to law at the operational level. It has become part of technical philosophy, in which few judges or practicing lawyers take any interest."[6] The problem with orthodox pragmatism stems from a problem with philosophy more generally. Philosophy, for Posner, has little of use to say about legal and political issues. Therefore, "appeals to pragmatism to guide adjudication and other governmental action should largely be cut loose from philosophy."[7] Moreover, it is foolish to expect judges or politicians to be schooled in philosophy.[8] Posner goes on to critique Richard Rorty, John Dewey, and other theorists he labels as "recusant" pragmatists who hope to "enable philosophers to make a constructive contribution to the solution of practical social problems, including legal problems."[9] Posner doubts the "feasibility of this quest."[10] The problem, in short, is philosophy, and Posner attempts to skim off the top of pragmatism several of its key ideas and discards the rest as philosophical fat.

The end product is "everyday pragmatism," a leaner, more useful, more practical pragmatism. As Posner describes it:

> Everyday pragmatism is the mindset denoted by the popular usage of the word "pragmatic," meaning practical and business-like, "no-nonsense," disdainful of abstract theory and intellectual pretension, contemptuous of moralizers and utopian dreamers.[11]

According to Posner, "[e]veryday pragmatists tend to be 'dry,' no-nonsense types. Philosophical pragmatists tend to be 'wets,' and to believe that somehow their philosophy really can clear the decks for liberal social policies, though this is largely an accident of the fact that John Dewey was a prominent liberal."[12] Pragmatism's "core is merely a disposition to base action on facts and consequences rather than on conceptualisms, generalities, pieties, and slogans."[13]

Posner observes that pragmatism "is not hostile to all theory. . . . [just] to the idea of using abstract moral and political theory to guide judicial decisionmaking."[14] The pragmatist "being unconcerned with maintaining law's conceptual autonomy and formalist pretensions, is more open to invasions of law from other provinces of thought than a more conventional legal thinker would be."[15] Thus, "theories that seek to guide empirical inquiry are welcomed in pragmatic adjudication."[16] Although the pragmatist is open-minded to insights from a variety of disciplines, she should be wary of philosophy, which for Posner is little more than "intellectual pretension" that isn't helpful in grappling with legal and policy issues.[17]

Therefore, the Posnerian pragmatist should reject philosophical theory as having no role to play in the law. Posner argues that "academic philosophy" is "a field that has essentially no audience among judges and lawyers—let alone among politicians—even when philosophy is taken up by law professors ... who think it *should* influence law."[18] Legal pragmatists reject "abstract theorizing of which professors of constitutional law are enamored, in which decisions are evaluated by reference to abstractions common in law talk such as fairness, justice, autonomy, and equality."[19] Further, Posner argues, when pragmatists examine a constitutional issue, such as "whether per-pupil expenditures on public school education should be equalized across school districts," the pragmatist avoids "question-begging vacuities (such as 'equality' and 'fundamental rights')."[20] "What sensible person," he asks "would be guided in such difficult, contentious, and fact-laden matters by a philosopher or his law-professor knock-off?"[21] According to Posner, "[p]ragmatism helps us see that the dream of using theory to guide and constrain political, including judicial, action is just that—a dream."[22]

In reaching these conclusions, Posner sets out pragmatically, but then veers off course. What begins as a pragmatic critique of theorizing in the clouds devolves into an attempt to quarantine philosophy from debates on the issues of the day. As I demonstrate below, this is hardly the relation between theory and practice the pragmatists had in mind. Moreover, pragmatism does not require us to discard abstract ideals such as "justice" or "equality." Nor does it have nothing to say about our normative ends. But if Posnerian pragmatism rings hollow and seems shallow, I will suggest that pragmatism amounts to much more.

PHILOSOPHY AND "INTELLECTUAL PRETENSION"

Posner's attempt to excise philosophy from pragmatism and from the law more generally is part of his ongoing quest to attack academic theorists. Posner is building on work from his 1999 book *The Problematics of Moral and Legal Theory*,[23] where he attacked legal and moral theory, and his 2002 book *Public Intellectuals: A Study of Decline*,[24] where he argued that public intellectuals serve little useful purpose. In *Law, Pragmatism, and Democracy*, Posner uses his notion of everyday pragmatism to argue that whereas other disciplines such as economics, sociology, and biology are useful in the law, philosophy is more of a hindrance than a help. According to Posner, academics are insulated from the "real" world and tend to become easily infatuated with empty abstractions such as justice, fairness, and equality.

One can readily understand Posner's concerns. Much theoretical academic work participates in a private conversation far removed from the pressing social problems of the day. Philosophical discourse, whether in academic philosophy or in legal theory, can be overly abstract, filled with jargon, and disconnected from current practice. The result is an insular world in an ivory tower, where academics talk mostly amongst themselves, producing a parade of half-baked ideas and impractical suggestions for reform.

In making this criticism, Posner echoes Dewey, who also staunchly criticized the academy for theorizing abstractly without attempting to connect theory to current practice. Dewey attacked theorizing that "becomes arbitrary, aloof—what is called 'abstract' when that word is used in a bad sense to designate something which exclusively occupies a realm of its own without contact with the things of ordinary experience."[25] Dewey criticized philosophy that attempted to treat itself as something more lofty than other forms of knowledge, as "a realm of higher Being" with "air purer than that in which exist the making and doing that relate to livelihood."[26] Like Dewey, Posner is right to criticize academic theorists who view their theorizing as a higher and purer activity than other disciplines that employ more empirical methods of analysis.

Dewey was critical of academic departments for creating pseudo-problems—taking problems from general experience and converting them into philosophical puzzles with a life of their own, disconnected from their origins in experience.[27] For Dewey, philosophy must begin in ordinary life with the concerns, pressures, and facts of contemporary existence. Indeed, philosophy is already caught up in contemporary political and social struggles:

When it is acknowledged that under disguise of dealing with ultimate reality, philosophy has been occupied with the previous values
embedded in social traditions, that it has sprung from a clash of
social ends and from a conflict of inherited institutions with incompatible contemporary tendencies, it will be seen that the task of the
future philosophy is to clarify men's ideas as to the social and moral
strifes of their own day.[28]

Philosophies that fail to do this often end up as both views from
nowhere and views that are going nowhere. For Dewey, "[p]hilosophy
recovers itself when it ceases to be a device for dealing with the problems of philosophers and becomes a method, cultivated by philosophers, for dealing with the problems of men."[29] Accordingly, Dewey
believed a "first-rate test" of the value of any philosophy consists in its
answer to this question:

Does it end in conclusions which, when they are referred back to
ordinary life-experience and their predicaments, render them more
significant, more luminous to us, and make our dealing with them
more fruitful?[30]

If a philosophy is to meet this challenge, it must take its starting
point from the problems of our everyday practices. Likewise a philosophy of law, as Dewey says, "cannot be set up as if it were a separate
entity, but can be discussed only in terms of the social conditions in
which it arises and of what it concretely does there."[31] Thus, Posner is
right to suggest that those interested in improving legal methods and
procedures should not look to academic philosophy or law departments for ready-made answers. He is also right to insist that constructive solutions usually require in-depth investigations of the facts.

However, Posner then takes too sharp a turn. He appears to equate
philosophy exclusively to the work of academic departments in universities, and then he rejects philosophy wholesale. In this way, he is like
many of Dewey's contemporaries who identified "education" narrowly
with instruction in schools. Dewey insisted that concern with education
—learning from experience to promote growth—is not the province of
one particular institution, but rather a broader concern at the heart
of many of our social institutions.[32] Education is not simply confined
to schools; it occurs in our conversations with each other, at work,

through the media, and through participation in public debate. Likewise, the practice of philosophy is much broader than the practice of
professors in academic institutions. Whether someone is a philosopher
is a function of the questions they ask and writing they do, rather than
whether they are employed by a philosophy department. For Dewey,
philosophy is not the exclusive domain of academic philosophers;
rather, it is the development of intelligent, critical, and reconstructive
methods for approaching the problems of lived experience. Philosophy
is something that everyone does or at least can do, not an insular club
that only those in the ivory tower can join. Therefore, Posner's concern
that the academic practice of philosophy is often overly technical and
disengaged from the problems of society is certainly not without merit,
but it doesn't imply that philosophy should be abandoned.[33]

THEORY AND PRACTICE

Posner is not alone in his view that pragmatists must abandon philosophical theorizing. Pragmatism is often criticized for being anti-
theoretical. For example, Steven Smith argues that "[l]egal pragmatism
is best understood as a kind of exhortation about theorizing."[34]

Without a role for philosophical theorizing, Posner's pragmatism
looks less to opportunities for criticism and reconstruction of un-
satisfactory practices, the two hallmarks of Deweyan pragmatic approach,[35] and more to opportunities for affirmation and acquiescence
to the status quo. Such an account of pragmatism leads critics like
David Luban to conclude that:

> Pragmatism represents in the arena of conceptual change what Burke
> represents in that of political change: a cautionary voice protesting
> those who seek to overthrow the amassed wisdom of generations on
> no better basis than the trifling speculations of philosophers.[36]

This account of pragmatism, as rejecting a role for philosophical
theory, stems in part from a misunderstanding of the pragmatic reconstruction of the theory and practice relationship. Under the traditional
model of the theory/practice relationship, philosophical theory is seen
as offering a blueprint for practice. One should learn the theory and
then put it into practice. But pragmatists, such as Dewey, never expected theory to guide practice in this way. Rather, Dewey sought to

make practice more intelligent and more critical. This does not require theoretical reason capable of determining its goals outside of historical practices; rather, it requires a critical and reconstructive approach to social institutions and practices. Indeed, as Thomas Grey notes, "thought always comes embodied in practices—culturally embedded habits and patterns of expectation, behavior, and response."[37]

Dewey was careful when discussing pragmatism not to establish necessary and sufficient conditions for calling something a pragmatic theory. Pragmatism did not emerge fully formed, but developed over time and will continue to develop as it is employed. It was initially conceived by Charles Peirce as a method for making ideas clear. Peirce held that if we had trouble determining the meaning of a concept, we should "consider what effects, which might conceivably have practical bearings, we conceive the object of our conception to have. Then, our conception of these effects is the whole of our conception of the object."[38] For Peirce, pragmatic inquiry was concerned exclusively with establishing the meaning of concepts. William James took Peirce's pragmatic attitude beyond a concern with establishing meaning to a concern with establishing truth and evaluating proposed courses of action based on their consequences.[39] Subsequently, Dewey developed a philosophy that aimed to reconstruct knowledge and social practices to better respond to the problems of the present.[40]

Calls to provide necessary and sufficient conditions for pragmatism, or to define pragmatism in isolation, risk converting it into the very positions it seeks to repudiate. In Dewey's considered view, it is "better to view pragmatism quite vaguely as part and parcel of a general movement of intellectual reconstruction."[41] Otherwise, pragmatism would have to be defined

> in terms of the very past systems against which it is a reaction; or, in escaping that alternative, to regard it as a fixed rival system making like claim to completeness and finality. And if, as I believe, one of the marked traits of the pragmatic movement is just the surrender of every such claim, how have we furthered our understanding of pragmatism?[42]

Thus, one can understand why Posner says that pragmatism is more a mood than a theory since pragmatism is not a theory of the traditional sort. Indeed, pragmatists view theories as tools. William

James famously claimed that in the hands of the pragmatist, "[t]heo-ries thus become instruments, not answers to enigmas, in which we can rest. . . . Pragmatism unstiffens all our theories, limbers them up and sets each one to work."[43] Philosophy doesn't define the proper ends of society, but is an ongoing effort to state the findings of past experi-ence. So it is puzzling when Posner insists that the judge will find nothing *in philosophy* to help her make her decision about "whether per-pupil expenditures on public school education should be equalized across school districts."[44] Indeed, there will probably be no ready-made answers, and certainly an investigation of different conceptions of "fairness," apart from developing a detailed grasp of present education and public finance policies, is unlikely to yield a good decision. But it is not clear why the extensive philosophical discussions of fairness would not be helpful. Indeed, such discussions take place not only in the ivory tower but in non-academic discourse—even in popular nov-els and movies.[45]

Posner does make an important observation when he insists that more work should be done in what he calls the "empirical lowlands."[46] As Posner observes: "The theoretical uplands, where democratic and judicial ideals are debated, tend to be arid and overgrazed; the empiri-cal lowlands are fertile but rarely cultivated."[47] The uplands are thus theoretical discourses that ask questions about the nature of justice, equality, and the good. The lowlands are efforts to explore empirically the results of our social practices. It is one thing to argue about the justification for policies such as affirmative action by sparring over competing conceptions of fairness, but equally important to the prag-matist is understanding the consequences of such rhetoric in practice. What results are produced by affirmative action policies?[48] Posner, like Dewey, thinks that theoretically minded individuals concerned with questions of justice and the like could accomplish much more by investigating these conceptions in the context of particular practices. Not only would they help to ameliorate present problems, but they would also be submitting their ideals to the test of experience. Indeed, law is an excellent field for the pragmatist since it provides a forum to investigate concretely the meaning of our ideals.

However, Posner's suspicion of abstract theoretical ideals leads him to insist that the everyday pragmatist stop discussing them. Yet, ironically, Posner himself characterizes pragmatism as "reasonableness" and without hesitation invokes the ideal of "freedom" as a guiding concern.[49]

Insofar as the language of "justice" has been dominated by the descendants of Kantian moralists who believe that our regulative ideals are the product of pure reason, then one can understand Posner's reservations. Dewey shared this concern.[50] For Dewey, terms like "justice" and "freedom" are not backed up by reference to Platonic forms, but are the products of our human experience and contested history.[51] We do not look to theory to tell us what "democracy," "justice," "equality," and "freedom" mean. We look to our experience of past practices. As Dewey observed, "we institute standards of justice, truth, esthetic quality, etc., in order that different objects and events may be so intelligently compared with one another as to give direction to activities dealing with concrete objects and affairs."[52]

The risk with Posner's no-abstraction strategy is that it silences meaningful community discussion. Terms such as "justice" and "equality" are not only used in the academy, but they are also part of popular social discourse. Many people talk about intrinsic goods and understand freedom as the ability to fulfill their desires.[53] Whereas Dewey offers us tools to reconstruct the meaning of these terms by giving priority to experience, Posner advises us to avoid the terms. The result may be that they remain to do mischief having been insulated from critical attention.

By eliminating philosophical theorizing, Posner discards pragmatic tools for transforming existing institutions, customs, and social norms. Pragmatism sees philosophy as critical inquiry that aims to unsettle status quo assumptions and then provide guidance for projects of social reconstruction. Dewey observed that we often act out of habit, which is an "an ability . . . formed through past experience."[54] Habits, for Dewey, "are conditions of intellectual efficiency."[55] While we need habit in order to function, habit can restrict the "reach" of our intellect; it can "fix its boundaries."[56] Habits are "blinders that confine the eyes of mind to the road ahead."[57] Social customs are "widespread uniformities of habit."[58] They "persist because individuals form their personal habits under conditions set by prior customs."[59] The problem with customs is that they can be "inert" and can readily lead "into conformity, constriction, surrender of scepticism and experiment."[60] The goal of philosophical inquiry is thus to make habits "more intelligent," by which Dewey means "more sensitively percipient, more informed with foresight, more aware of what they are about, more direct and sincere, more flexibly responsive than those now current."[61] Rather than be controlled by habit and custom, we must strive toward the intelligent control of habit.[62] This involves criticizing current institutions and finding ways to reconstruct them.

Of course, Dewey observed, we cannot abandon our institutions, as this would lead to "chaos and anarchy"; rather, we must "make over these institutions so that they serve under changing conditions."[63] "[T]o maintain the institutions unchanged is death and fossilization."[64] In *Experience and Nature*, Dewey agreed with Justice Holmes, who said that we must try "to make our desires intelligent. The trouble is that our ideals for the most part are inarticulate, and that even if we have made them definite we have very little experimental knowledge of the way to bring them about."[65] Making our desires and ideas "articulate" is "criticism," says Dewey, "and when carried on in the grand manner, philosophy."[66]

Therefore, far from being a form of anti-philosophical empiricism, pragmatic method is a theoretical and critical enterprise. To the extent that pragmatism is an "attitude," it is one that is radical, for it is skeptical, experimental, and restless. The pragmatic temperament is one that is constantly prodding and questioning; it focuses on change and transformation. Although the pragmatist need not be committed to radical ends, she must be committed to a radical kind of criticism and experimentation. This doesn't mean that pragmatism must reject the status quo; but it does mean that the pragmatist must be wary of accepting inherited ends uncritically. Far from mundane and banal, pragmatism attempts to escape from the blinders of existing habits, customs, and conventions; it attempts to question accepted beliefs and "truths." The result of this attitude is a critical edge, one with a bit of zing to it. This is a far cry from Posner's everyday pragmatist, who appears to be rather conventional and complacent, who sticks to "just the facts" and who evaluates situations with hard-nosed "common sense."

MEANS AND ENDS

Posner's thin account of pragmatism runs into serious problems when it comes to offering guidance concerning the normative ends we should adopt. These problems emerge most explicitly when Posner discusses how the pragmatic judge should adjudicate cases. In articulating his account of pragmatic adjudication, he views pragmatism as a method that is helpful in analyzing whether the means we select can further our ends. But it has little to say about the normative ends we choose to adopt. Critics of pragmatism often attack pragmatism on this basis, viewing it as empty. Pragmatism, on this account, is nothing more than a tool that can be used by anybody to achieve whatever ends they have in mind. But as I illustrate below, a thicker account of pragmatism reveals that it is much more than this.

Posner begins his account of pragmatic adjudication by defending against charges that it counsels judges to ignore precedent and decide cases simply based upon one's personal views about the best outcome. Ronald Dworkin, legal pragmatism's well-known nemesis, argues that pragmatism is disrespectful of the past in general, and precedent in particular. In *Law's Empire,* he writes that the "pragmatist thinks judges should always do the best they can for the future, in the circumstances, unchecked by any need to respect or secure consistency in principle with what other officials have done or will do.[67] Dworkin views the pragmatist as focused almost exclusively on short-term expediency, and he is not alone in this view.[68]

Posner emphatically and correctly rejects this account of pragmatic adjudication. He notes that it is true that the pragmatist judge doesn't feel any special duty to follow precedent: "The pragmatist values continuity with past enactments and decisions, but because such continuity is indeed a social value, not because he feels a sense of duty to the past."[69] But this does not imply that the pragmatist will simply do whatever she pleases, without any respect for precedent. Rather, "[l]egal pragmatism is forward-looking, regarding adherence to past decisions as a (qualified) necessity rather than as an ethical duty."[70] Posner correctly contends that the pragmatist has instrumental reasons for adhering to precedent. Failure to follow precedent will undermine the stability of the legal system, which depends upon predictability and fairness (understood as treating like cases like).[71] Moreover, past decisions may helpfully inform our present investigations. Thus, Dworkin and other critics of pragmatic adjudication fail to recognize that the pragmatist has good reasons to respect precedent.

Further, Posner argues that pragmatism is not merely *ad hoc* decisionmaking:

> Pragmatic adjudication is not, as its ill-wishers charge, a synonym for ad hoc decisionmaking, that is for always deciding a case in the way that will have the best immediate consequences. Such an approach would be unpragmatic in disregarding the adverse systemic consequences of ad hoc adjudication.[72]

In other words, concludes Posner, " '[s]hortsighted' is not part of the definition of 'pragmatic.' "[73]

Nevertheless, despite Posner's strong dispute with critics such as Dworkin, they *all* share a similar impoverished notion of pragmatism. After Posner refutes the argument that judges should respect precedent for its own sake, he then goes too far in the other direction. He argues that "the past is a repository of useful information, but it has no claim on us. The criterion of whether we should adhere to past practices is the consequences of doing so for now and the future."[74] Posner's insistence that the past has no claim on us is problematic, especially in our constitutional democracy. It conjures up images of the judge arriving on a scene armed with a storehouse of "facts" from the past, then rendering her choice in light of whatever ends she has in mind. The origin of these ends apparently doesn't need to be accounted for. Dworkin therefore has a valid criticism when he argues that for adjudication in a constitutional democracy, these ends *do* need to be accounted for. Thus, both Posner and Dworkin view the pragmatist judge as deciding according to unjustified ends.

Although Posner does recognize that the pragmatic judge must determine which consequences "are good and which bad, let alone how much weight to place on each consequence," and that "goodness and badness are to be determined by reference to human needs and interests," he also suggests that "nothing in consequentialism or pragmatism helps to determine them."[75] Therefore, "different judges, each with his own idea of the community's needs and interests will weigh consequences differently."[76] The solution is thus a diverse judiciary because "[s]uch a judiciary is more representative, and its decisions will therefore command greater acceptance in a diverse society than would the decisions of a mandarin court."[77]

If pragmatism can't help us assess the goodness and badness of our ends, then it seems fair to say that the pragmatist simply accepts (or inherits) his ends uncritically. This reduces the contribution of pragmatism to merely aiding the selection of means to achieve particular ends. When asked about which ends to choose, the pragmatist has nothing to say.[78] For Posner, pragmatism is value-neutral and "lack[s] a moral compass."[79] This account of pragmatism is shared by many neo-pragmatists as well as their critics. For example, Brian Tamanaha has stated that "pragmatism is empty of substance,"[80] and he contends that "[p]ragmatism does not say what the good is, how to live, what economic or political system to develop, or anything else of that nature."[81] Lynn Baker's critique of the pragmatism of Richard Rorty has in mind a similar account of pragmatism:

> In the end, pragmatism appears to be useful in achieving progressive social change to the extent that one profits from statements such as, "There is no method or procedure to be followed except courageous and imaginative experimentation." Or, as the Nike people say, "Just do it."[82]

This is the account of pragmatism that Dworkin critiques, and rightly so. We must justify the legitimacy of the ends we select to guide our adjudication. Since citizens do not vote on every issue, and since we are bound by a Constitution which circumscribes our ordinary law-making, judges need to explain at least two things: (1) why they believe that one set of ends provides a better account of who we are as a people; and (2) what the implications of that account are for the present problems we face and our choices about who we as a people will become.

However, although Dworkin's concerns have merit, his critique is misplaced when he speaks of pragmatism more generally beyond Posner's account. If the pragmatist simply treats the selection of ends as the product of a judge's individual choice, this effectively insulates those ends from critical scrutiny and is markedly unpragmatic. Pragmatism *does* demand the critical assessment of our ends. Where did they come from? What conditions were they responding to? What have been the results? Who has benefited from their adoption? Who has suffered? Have they been democratically selected?

Therefore, the pragmatist would understand that any view of the best future must be informed by a view of who we are as a people—and this depends upon an interpretation of our history.[83] As Justice Holmes correctly noted, the obligation to history is not a duty (as Dworkin would have it), but a necessity.[84] Pragmatists recognize that ends are not ahistorical. Dewey noted that "personal desire and belief are functions of habit and custom."[85] We do not get our ends from some *a priori* source; they emerge from experience. And our values originate not just from our own experience, but from collective social experience, which has a long history and is embodied in our current habits, customs, and traditions. In this way, the past perpetuates itself; it has a hold on us.[86] We cannot simply wipe the slate clean or assume a "tabula rasa in order to permit the creation of a new order."[87] We adopt the ends we do often because they are transmitted to us by our parents, education, and culture. As Dewey warned, many of our ends "have come to us through unexamined customs, [or] uncriticized tradition."[88] Since ends do not emerge from some transcendent realm of pure truth, the pragmatist does not simply accept her own ends uncritically. She must subject them to critical inquiry. Criticism "occurs whenever a moment is devoted to looking to see what sort of value is present; whenever instead of accepting a value-object wholeheartedly, being rapt by it, we raise even a shadow of a question about its worthy, or modify our sense of it by even a passing estimate of its probable future."[89] This involves understanding the origins of our ends, the reasons for their existence, and whether these reasons still hold true today. Through pragmatic criticism, we may discover that particular ends have merely survived through inertia or that the reasons for their existence no longer apply to our present situation.

As Dewey argued, we "must take the history of any intuition or attitude of moral consciousness in both directions: *both ex parte ante* and *ex parte post*. We must consider it with reference to the antecedents which evoked it, and with reference to its later career and fate."[90] We must look to the genesis of a particular end because:

> It arises in a certain context, and as a reaction to certain circumstances; it has a subsequent history which can be traced. It maintains and reinforces certain conditions, and modifies others. It becomes a stimulus which provokes new modes of action. Now when we see

how and why the belief came about, and also know what else came about because of it, we have a hold upon the worth of the belief which is entirely wanting when we set it up as an isolated intuition.[91]

Certainly, Posner as a pragmatist does not argue that we should embrace ahistorical ends or claim that our visions of the best future are unconnected to the past. Indeed, he tells us that "commercial values . . . have, since almost the beginning, largely defined American society," a conclusion presumably informed by historical observation.[92] But these insights into our values are just interjected into the discussion as obvious conclusions. Where do these conclusions come from? Presumably, they emerge from a pragmatic analysis of past experience. But rather than make the case for his historical interpretation and consider competing interpretations, as the pragmatist would, Posner is content to simply state his intuitions. Of course, we might forgive him for not giving us a detailed analysis in a book filled with many insights and already nearly four hundred pages long. And even for someone who writes on complex topics as quickly as Posner, there are only twenty-four hours in a day, and not every point can be fully developed.

But Posner is mistaken when he proposes that there is nothing useful to be done in terms of critically assessing our present value commitments. Posner appears to view one's ends as similar to mere tastes. As discussed earlier in this chapter, Posner has rejected any attempt to use philosophical theory to justify our ends, since philosophy for Posner is nothing but appealing to pure abstract ideals. Therefore, Posner doesn't seem to believe that discussion about our ends will be fruitful—perhaps even analogous to arguing over whether chocolate is better than vanilla. This is why Posner ultimately recommends a diverse judiciary—at least, different ends can be represented even if discussing them won't lead us anywhere.

But the pragmatist does have something to say about our ends. The pragmatist justifies her value commitments by analyzing their historical genesis. Guiding ideals such as "fairness," "justice," and "freedom" must be critically examined by looking to past experience. Posner complains that such ideals are empty abstractions, useless for assisting us in decisions.[93] Yet they are rendered useless not because they are abstractions, but because insufficient effort is made to critically explore their genesis.

Therefore, the pragmatist is committed to finding substantive sustenance for her guiding ideals through experiential inquiry. This requires difficult historical investigation and interpretation. There is no guarantee that one account will emerge as superior to all others, although many accounts, upon careful investigation, are shown to be wanting. If a particular view of justice or democracy is to be favored, it should be favored because of its past consequences and future consequences. Those in disagreement over political ends need not refrain from invoking considerations of justice, freedom, equality, and democracy, but they must not let matters rest there. They must explain the experiential basis for their choices. Given an assessment of our past experiences and practices, why should we prefer an account of democracy that tries to increase the participation of all citizens? Or, alternatively, why should we prefer to minimize the participation of most citizens? These are the discussions we need to have.

Under this view, the pragmatist need not be a shallow empiricist who has something to say about means but nothing much to say about ends. The pragmatist need not eschew philosophical theorizing or discussion of regulative ideals. Far from being a mere method that provides little guidance as to our normative ends, pragmatism enables us to have philosophical debates about them in ways that avoid appealing to hollow, transcendent abstractions. Pragmatism is thus an invitation to a different kind of debate, a debate that the Posnerian pragmatist ignores.

IMPLICATIONS OF LEGAL PRAGMATISM

In a number of examples sprinkled throughout *Law, Pragmatism and Democracy*, Posner attempts to demonstrate how his legal pragmatism works in practice by addressing specific legal issues and topics. In many instances, Posner claims that his conclusions are pragmatic, but this characterization becomes dubious when his reasoning is considered more carefully. A few of these examples demonstrate that Posner's reasoning does not embody the attributes of pragmatic analysis, and in many cases Posner fails even on his own pragmatic terms. The point of examining these examples is not to engage in a direct debate with Posner over his conclusions, but to critique the way Posner goes about reaching his conclusions, his method of reasoning and analysis.

JUDICIAL RESTRAINT VS. JUDICIAL ACTIVISM

At one point in the book, Posner says that an "implication for law of Dewey's epistemology is that courts should either have no power to invalidate legislation or exercise it in only extreme circumstances, when faced by a law patently unconstitutional or utterly appalling."[94] This is the language of judicial restraint, and Posner is alluding to Justice Holmes' famous "puke test," in which only laws so despicable that they make one puke should be held unconstitutional.[95]

For Posner, by "invalidating legislation, courts prevent political experimentation."[96] "In Dewey's intellectual universe, invalidating a statute is not just checking a political preference. It is profoundly rather than merely superficially undemocratic. . . . It places expert opinion over the distributed intelligence of the mass of people and prevents the emergence of the best policies through intellectual natural selection."[97] As a result, "[c]ontemporary Deweyans who advocate judicial adoption of the current left-liberal political agenda, bypassing legislatures, can have little respect for distributed intelligence, democratic diversity, or social experimentation."[98] Thus Posner argues that Deweyan pragmatists on their own terms must support judicial restraint.

This conclusion is false. In contrast to Posner, who speaks in a generalized ahistorical manner, the Deweyan pragmatist would be reluctant to conclude that judicial restraint, or any judicial style, would be better at all times in our history. Holmes judged at a different point during our history; perhaps in his time judicial restraint was a pragmatic response. But it certainly does not mean that judicial restraint is always demanded by pragmatism. To justify judicial restraint, the pragmatist would examine why it is best *at this particular point in our history.* Ironically, just a few pages earlier in the book, Posner seems to recognize this point. He extols Chief Justice John Marshall as an exemplar of pragmatism in judging.[99] Posner defends Marshall against attacks that he was too formalistic and relied more on rhetoric than reason.[100] "Marshall created judicial review as a pragmatic response to the inevitable crisis over the role of the judiciary in the constitutional scheme."[101] Marshall, whose judicial style certainly cannot be labeled as judicial restraint, nevertheless was pragmatic because he had an "extraordinary fit" with his times."[102] If Posner is correct about Marshall, then it certainly does not follow that the pragmatist should favor judicial restraint over activism in principle. Instead, if Posner were to argue pragmatically for judicial restraint, he would need to justify why, based upon past experience and an analysis of our current problems, restraint is the most appropriate response at this time in our history. In light of the analysis of Marshall, one would expect Posner to recognize that restraint might not be appropriate in all contexts, for all cases.

Posner's argument seems to be that since pragmatism advocates for experimentation in general, this means that pragmatists should defer to legislative experimentation. However, even if one were to accept the commitment to experimentation at face value, it would not follow that judicial experimentation should be ruled out. In important respects, *Brown v. Board of Education*[103] can be viewed as a judicial experiment rather than the blocking of experimentation.

Beyond this, one must be careful not to turn Dewey's commitment to experimentalism into its opposite. Dewey's claim is that scientific methods work better for grappling with our problems than adherence to absolutes. It would be ironic to maintain an absolutist commitment to experimentation in the name of pragmatism. The fact that pragmatists recognize virtues of experimental methods does not mean they endorse experimentation in all forms and contexts. The pragmatic commitment to experimentation, for example, does not lead pragmatists to favor Nazi experimentation on humans. Pragmatism is a commitment to an experimental method, one that keeps testing its conclusions in experience. It is not a commitment to experimentation for its own sake.

Striking down a law, even one that is "experimental," can still be a pragmatic response. For example, legislatures can fail to be democratic. As Posner himself recognizes, interest groups can have an overly strong influence on legislation.[104] Or legislatures can fail to adopt the appropriate means to achieve the stated end of a law.[105] Judges, in part due to the relatively insulated nature of the judiciary, can subject laws to critical scrutiny when powerful lobbies seek to prevent legislatures from doing so. As Daniel Solove has noted, the judiciary has the potential "to make institutions more democratic and humane, to force officials to base their policies on the best empirical research of the day, to be guided by democratic values, to be more humble and skeptical of their own practices."[106] Additionally, Daniel Farber observes that "[f]or the pragmatist, . . . the question of the advisability of judicial review turns on its usefulness for promoting a flourishing democratic society—democratic not just in the sense of ballot casting but also in the sense that citizens are in charge of the intelligent development of their lives."[107] Thus, both judicial activism and restraint can be pragmatic, even democratic, responses to the problems of the present.

LIBERTY VS. SECURITY

Posner also applies his pragmatism to an extensive discussion of civil liberties and security.[108] Posner contends that civil libertarians are unpragmatic when they treat "our existing civil liberties—protections of privacy, of the freedom of the press, of the rights of criminal suspects, and the rest—as sacrosanct and insisting therefore that the battle against international terrorism must accommodate itself to them."[109] Posner engages in a cost-benefit analysis between liberty and security, and he concludes: "A pragmatist would say [civil liberties] *should* be curtailed to the extent that the beneficial consequences for the safety of the nation . . . outweigh the adverse impact on liberty."[110] History demonstrates that government officials have not exaggerated security dangers but in fact have "disastrously underestimated these dangers."[111] Echoing Chief Justice Rehnquist, Posner argues that although civil liberties should be "curtailed in time of war or other national emergency," civil libertarians wrongly fear that this curtailment will serve as a "precedent in time of peace."[112] Posner writes:

> The events of September 11 revealed the United States to be in greater jeopardy from international terrorism than had been believed by most people until then. . . . It stands to reason that such a revelation would lead to our civil liberties being curtailed.[113]

Posner criticizes civil libertarians for treating existing civil liberties "as sacrosanct."[114] He seems to be suggesting that civil libertarians are unpragmatic because they adhere to rights as absolutes. However, Posner attacks a caricature of the civil libertarian argument, viewing liberties as absolute. Many civil libertarians are pragmatists, not absolutists.

Posner also attacks civil libertarians when they offer "historical examples of supposed overreactions to threats to national security."[115] In contrast, Posner argues against the claim that "the lesson of history is that officials habitually exaggerate dangers to the nation's security."[116] He elaborates:

Actually, the lesson of history is the opposite. Officialdom has repeatedly and disastrously underestimated these dangers—whether it is the danger of secession that led to the Civil War, or the danger of a Japanese attack on the United States that led to the disaster at Pearl Harbor, or the danger of Soviet espionage in the 1940s that accelerated the Soviet Union's acquisition of nuclear weapons and by doing so emboldened Stalin to encourage North Korea to invade South Korea in 1950 or the installation in 1962 of Soviet missiles in Cuba that precipitated the Cuban missile crisis, or the outbreaks of urban violence and political assassinations in the 1960s, or the Tet Offensive of 1968 in the Vietnam War, or the Iranian Revolution of 1979 and subsequent taking of American diplomats hostage, or the catastrophe of September 11, 2001.[117]

However, these examples do not involve a tradeoff between liberty and security. They are failures of foreign intelligence or political judgment. The point of the civil libertarians is that the government has often overreacted in curtailing liberty in times of crisis. Posner's examples involve the failure to anticipate security threats. Without demonstrating how curtailing liberty has improved our ability to avert these events, Posner's examples have little relevance.

Posner then contends that to the extent that the government overreacted by curtailing liberty in times of crisis, this should not be a great concern since "[t]he curtailment of civil liberties in the Civil War, World War I (and the ensuing 'Red Scare'), World War II, and the Cold War did not outlast the emergencies."[118] But curtailments of liberties harmed thousands of innocent citizens, sometimes quite severely. Just because the government eventually realizes it overreacted and apologizes does not set everything right. Apologies are meaningful when they guide future action. In light of a history marred by frequent misguided responses to threats, a pragmatic response would counsel caution. For example, from 1919 to 1920, the government rounded up more than 10,000 suspected communists, many without warrants.[119] This became known as the Palmer Raids or "Red Scare." The raids were a reaction to fear over communists, anarchists, and labor unrest.[120] They began in 1919 when the home of Attorney General A. Mitchell Palmer was bombed.[121] Soon after this, bombs were detonated in eight other cities. Letter bombs were mailed to many elites, but most were stopped at the post office due to inadequate postage.[122] After being rounded up, people were deported, often based exclusively on membership in certain organizations.[123]

In 1942, in the name of national security, the government rounded up around 120,000 people of Japanese descent living on the West Coast and imprisoned them in internment camps.[124] In a series of cases, including *Korematsu v. United States*,[125] the Supreme Court upheld the internment as constitutional under "most rigid scrutiny."[126] Few today would defend *Korematsu*, but Posner, who is candid and unafraid to take controversial positions, appears to support it. He asks: "If the Constitution is not to be treated as a suicide pact, why should military exigencies not influence the scope of the constitutional rights that the Supreme Court has manufactured from the Constitution's vague provisions?"[127]

However, the internment has long been acknowledged to have been a terrible mistake. Even the United States government has formally apologized.[128] Posner contends, however, that we must be wary of lessons we draw from the 20/20 vision of hindsight. Just because the government's fears that Japanese Americans were engaged in dangerous acts of espionage later proved to be false does not mean that at the time of the internment the government was unjustified in taking action. But this does not imply that we must privilege the fears of the moment. On the contrary, as emergency workers and soldiers well know, we must take the lessons of the past to guide us in developing our habits for facing the future. Pragmatism aims to improve future decisions by learning from past ones. This is why the pragmatist studies past experience—to find out what worked and what failed, and to chart a better course for the future.

Beyond the internment, the McCarthy-era hunt for communists during the 1950s has been shown to have been a severe overreaction. Recently released transcripts of secret Senate hearings suggest that McCarthy may have deliberately misled the public about the threat.[129] The anti-communist movement resulted in terrible harm to many individuals. People labeled as communists lost their jobs and were blacklisted from employment.[130] Individuals exposed as communists faced retaliation in the private sector, with numerous journalists, professors, entertainers, and others fired from their jobs and blacklisted from future employment.[131] Ellen Schrecker notes that federal agencies exaggerated "the danger of radicalism" because of the "desire to present themselves as protecting the community against the threat of internal subversion."[132] Historians also argue that the anti-communist movement was not merely a response to security concerns, but a means for carrying out the right-wing agendas of opportunistic politicians.[133]

In his most recent book, *Not a Suicide Pact,* Posner articulates his position in greater detail. He explicitly recognizes that the internment of 100,000 Japanese residents was based on "groundless suspicion" and classifies the interned as "innocent victims." He also notes that "a number of harmless members of the Communist Party lost their jobs during the McCarthy period."[134] This is a helpful clarification of his underlying views from the earlier work because Posner now makes clear that it is appropriate to count these events as costs. Despite Posner's more nuanced description, however, his surface message remains the same. Though we may recognize that "curtailing civil liberties imposes costs,"[135] the relevant question is "whether the costs exceed the benefits." It appears that Posner still thinks these costs were worth incurring. Posner opines: "Civil libertarians tend to exaggerate the costs (how many innocent U.S. citizens in a population of 300 million have experienced real hardship as a result of the post–9/11 security measures?) and to ignore or slight the benefits."[136] Though Posner is certainly right that one cannot look at costs in a vacuum which excludes consideration of benefits, it is not enough to ask whether benefits exceed costs. We must ask whether the tradeoff is inevitable and whether we can do better. Even if the benefits outweigh the costs, assuming the costs are severe, we must certainly strive to reduce them if they are unnecessary for achieving the benefit. The pragmatist seeks to avoid the mistakes of harming innocents from occurring again; she does not view such mistakes as inevitable. She studies the past to see if there are better ways to identify the true threats from the manufactured ones. In the past, government officials have seized upon fears of national security to pursue their own personal agendas and prejudices. At the very least, an examination of our history should make us more guarded and skeptical when the government seeks to eliminate liberty in the name of security.

Many public intellectuals made such a response when, after September 11, the government rounded up thousands of people, restricted attorney-client confidentiality, instituted military tribunals, secretly detained and interrogated people, and increased electronic surveillance. Posner, however, condemns the critics of these measures such as Bruce Ackerman, Jeffrey Rosen, Michael Dorf, Ronald Dworkin, and Jack Balkin for being unpragmatic.[137] He criticizes them because legal thinkers simply lack the expertise to understand international terrorism and to adequately assess the security risks. In *Not a Suicide Pact,* Posner says more about his underlying idea: "Most civil libertarians, and almost all their leaders, are lawyers. They are comfortable defending liberties recognized by law but uncomfortable assessing threats to national security, about which they know little and don't want to learn more. Liberty, they think, is part of law, is something therefore within their ken; national security is not. That is why, rather than becoming national security mavens, civil liberties lawyers are content to narrate a history of civil liberties violations."[138] But Posner's own position, which appears to have softened a bit since *Law, Pragmatism and Democracy,* still amounts to little more than an abstract claim stating that liberty must be sacrificed to protect security.

Posner appears to assume that liberty and security must be mutually exclusive, an assumption that may not entirely be correct. Indeed, historically, America has remained quite safe and secure despite its tradition of civil liberties. Might our tradition of civil liberties *contribute* to our safety? Not only may curtailments of liberty bring us no greater security, they in fact might lead to less security.[139] The pragmatist would certainly entertain this question and would not be so fast to assume a dichotomous tradeoff between liberty and security.

In fact, following the historical pattern, the government has recently confessed that it overreacted after September 11 and improperly rounded up numerous individuals.[140] For Posner, this does not present much of a problem because life will eventually return to normal; overreaction is just what happens in times of crisis. But the pragmatist would not confuse excuse for explanation. She would look to history and think about how we could better grapple with crises and the tendency to respond with misguided measures that often involve the use of racial and ethnic categories.

GENERAL VS. AD HOC APPROACHES TO THE FOURTH AMENDMENT

Posner also discusses another startling implication of his pragmatism. Making an argument similar to that of Akhil Amar,[141] Posner contends that the word "unreasonable" in the Fourth Amendment "invites a wide-ranging comparison between the benefits and costs of a search or seizure."[142] This is in contrast to the current approach to the Fourth Amendment, where searches and seizures, regardless of their benefits, are subject to the requirement that government officials obtain a warrant supported by probable cause. To obtain a warrant, law enforcement officials must go before a neutral judge or magistrate and demonstrate that "the facts and circumstances within [the police's] knowledge and of which they had reasonably trustworthy information [are] sufficient in themselves to warrant a man of reasonable caution in the belief that an offense has been or is being committed."[143] Posner argues that a more pragmatic approach to the Fourth Amendment would adopt a "sliding scale" where "the level of suspicion required to justify the search or seizure should fall . . . as the magnitude of the crime under investigation rises."[144] Posner views his approach as pragmatic because it eschews absolutes and engages in ad hoc balancing.

However, Posner fails to justify on pragmatic terms why a sliding-scale approach is preferable to the more general rule of requiring warrants supported by probable cause. Posner seems to view his sliding-scale approach as better than a more generalized approach because it is more contextual. Although certainly the pragmatist cares about context, this doesn't mean that the pragmatist always adopts an ad hoc approach. As Posner himself argues earlier, decision according to rule is not necessarily unpragmatic, since "the loss from ignoring consequences in the particular case must be balanced against the gain from simplifying inquiry, minimizing judicial discretion, increasing the transparency of law, and making legal obligation more definite."[145] Posner supplies no reason why this argument does not apply in the context of Fourth Amendment adjudication.

A generalized warrant rule can certainly be justified pragmatically. Warrants serve as a check on the power of the executive branch. In fact, the founders adopted the Fourth Amendment in order to limit executive power.[146] Warrants force law enforcement officials to justify their exercises of power.[147] As Justice Douglas explained for the Court,

> We are not dealing with formalities. The presence of a search warrant serves a high function. Absent some grave emergency, the Fourth Amendment has interposed a magistrate between the citizen and the

police. This was done not to shield criminals nor to make the home a safe place for illegal activities. It was done so that an objective mind might weigh the need to invade that privacy in order to enforce the law. The right of privacy was deemed too precious to entrust to the discretion of those whose job is the detection of crime and the arrest of criminals. Power is a deadly thing; and history shows that the police acting on their own cannot be trusted. And so the Constitution requires a magistrate to pass on the desires of the police before they violate the privacy of the home.[148]

The Fourth Amendment's requirement that the government demonstrate that there be individualized suspicion protects against the risk that innocent people will be searched by mistake. It also prevents the government from engaging in "fishing expeditions."[149] This is why a warrant must describe with "particular[ity] . . . the place to be searched and the persons or things to be seized."[150] The Fourth Amendment was inspired by the framers' experience with general warrants and writs of assistance.[151] These devices permitted "sweeping searches and seizures without any evidentiary basis."[152] The framers believed that allowing the government to engage in such searches was too threatening to liberty, for it could easily become a tool to attack people for their political views.[153]

The pragmatist might conclude that these goals cannot be readily achieved by a more contextualized rule. The point is not that pragmatism supports a generalized or ad hoc approach to the Fourth Amendment. Rather, the point is that the analysis, even on Posner's own terms, should take a different form. The question is not one of whether standards are, in principle, more pragmatic than rules. Attempts to solve such quandaries in theory risk subverting our ability to make pragmatic decisions in practice. We must instead compare the consequences of the respective approaches in our efforts to decide which is more desirable. This is what pragmatism recommends.

DEWEY, PRAGMATISM, AND DEMOCRACY

Posner's contention that Dewey's political views "have no organic relation to his philosophy"[154] is false. In fact, Dewey's theory of democracy is deeply connected to his pragmatism. Dewey's pragmatism was one that recognized that flux and change are a large part of experience. We live in a world of risk, uncertainty, hazard, and unpredictability.[155] We crave certainty, regularity, and stability. Philosophical reflection begins from problems and confusion; its aim is to clarify.[156] Thus, philosophy begins as a way to cope with the uncertainty of experience. The problem was that philosophy developed a tendency, once it had clarified, to dismiss the confusion and replace it with the clarified as the true antecedent reality.[157] Modern epistemology, according to Dewey, was an attempt to deny the "temporal quality" to reality, to reject change and flux.[158]

The "experimental method" of pragmatism, one that Posner extols, is Dewey's response to the question about how to cope with change. "Constant revision is the work of experimental inquiry."[159] According to Dewey, philosophy can contribute to the aim of "the richest and fullest experience possible" through criticism which helps not only clarify the coherence of our intellectual ideals, but make manifest the consequences of our actions.[160]

Dewey's democratic theory is in large part merely a broader application of his pragmatism. The traits of Deweyan democracy—openness, participatory, transformative, future-directed, experimental, radical—are all part of the pragmatic method of inquiry. Democracy is thus also a commitment to a form of inquiry—or, in other words, the endorsement of experimental method on the social and political stage.

For Dewey, democracy is "a way of life, social and individual."[161] Democracy is thus a way to embody the experimental method in the way we govern ourselves. As Hilary Putnam observes, for Dewey, democracy is "not just a form of social life, among other workable forms of social life; it is a precondition for the full application of intelligence to the solution of social problems."[162] As Dewey wrote: "[D]emocracy is much broader than a special political form, a method of conducting government, of making laws and carrying on governmental administration by means of popular suffrage and elected officers."[163]

John Stuhr explains Dewey's conception of democracy as "a form of *life* rather than a form of *government* alone."[164] Democratic government is "a means for realizing democratic ends in individual lives and social relationships."[165] Under this view, democracy does not primarily consist of institutions or government structures. As Stuhr observes:

> Democracy exists only on paper and in statute unless individuals enact it in their own transactions day by day and face-to-face in local communities. That is, a society of individuals can become a democracy only as those individuals act democratically.[166]

Thus, even if our government has a democratic form, we are not democratic unless "people's actual lives and social relations" are democratic.[167] In this way, we cannot "treat democracy in America as a done deed, finished and final."[168] Democracy is an unfinished endeavor. As Stuhr notes, we must "reconstruct our institutions to accomplish democracy over again for our own time."[169] In Dewey's words, democracy is not a thing that can be "handed on from one person or generation to another."[170] It is a way of living.

Democracy, for Dewey, is participatory. As William Caspary observes, "Dewey is, above all, a participatory democratic theorist."[171] According to Dewey, citizens must have "a responsible share according to capacity in shaping the aims and policies of the groups to which one belongs."[172] Under Dewey's theory, participation is valuable in and of itself. For Posner, participation has no value unless it can achieve results that benefit one's self-interests.

Beyond being valuable in and of itself, participation is valuable instrumentally as well. According to Dewey, self-government "is educative," for it "forces recognition that there are common interests."[173] Thus, the purpose of democracy is not to take the people as they are. The value of democratic participation is to educate people, to enable them to realize common interests and see themselves as part of a community.

Unlike Posner's characterization of Dewey as a proponent of a highly sophisticated concept of deliberative democracy, Dewey's theory of participatory democracy does not require that people engage in a academically rigorous discourse; rather, it requires that people participate in a discussion of the meaning of ideals understood in the context of present circumstances. These are philosophical discussions not because they take place in universities, but because they ask about the good life under present social conditions. Dewey understood democracy as both a means and an end: "The fundamental principle of democracy is that the ends of freedom and individuality for all can be attained only by means that accord with those ends."[174]

It's important not to confuse Dewey's call to involve the whole community in the determination of its guiding ideals with the claim that there is no role for "experts" in our democracy. For Posner, reliance on expertise is contrary to the participatory nature of Deweyan democracy: "[D]oubting that anyone has a handle on the really big truths, especially those of a moral, religious, or political casts, pragmatists are inclined to throw up their hands and say, let the people decide such matters because there are no trustworthy experts on them."[175] On the contrary, Dewey's democratic theory does not require abandoning a role for experts in government. As Westbrook notes, Dewey "firmly believed that experts performed indispensable functions in complex societies, he explicitly consigned them to an advisory role and advocated the subordination of expert administration to fully participatory, deliberative democratic politics."[176] Experts are needed to help the larger community understand the choices available and their consequences, but they are not needed to decide on behalf of the community what is best for them.

Is Deweyan democracy too idealistic? For Posner, pragmatism demands a firm grounding in current "reality." Although the pragmatist is certainly mindful of the way things currently are, Posner misunderstands pragmatism's stance toward the current reality. Philosophy must begin in experience and relate back to experience. Dewey criticized non-empirical method as starting from the world of theory.[177] In contrast, "empirical method sets out from the actual subject-matter of primary experience."[178] But this does not mean that the pragmatist takes primary experience as given and immutable. The pragmatist focuses on the possibility of change. What keeps the pragmatist grounded is not a tough-minded empiricism that is tethered to facts, but a recognition that philosophical inquiry begins and ends with primary experience. In other words, philosophical inquiry emerges from primary experience, not from some prior transcendent reality, and philosophy is pursued instrumentally—to deal with the problems of experience—not for its own sake. Hence, Dewey argued that the results of philosophical inquiry must return to "actual experience," where they can be tested out, rather than remain "curiosities to be deposited . . . in a metaphysical museum."[179] This is not the same as the claims of the empiricists or realists who focus almost exclusively on privileging the ability of primary experience to speak for itself and denigrating the role of theory. Thus, as discussed earlier, pragmatism is a way to reconstruct the theory/practice relationship; it is not a rejection of theory. As James saw it, pragmatism is a middle-way.

Pragmatism is oriented toward the future. This does not mean that understanding the current state of affairs and how we got there historically isn't important. On the contrary, it is of utmost importance. But pragmatism looks to how we solve problems; it is forward-looking. The pragmatist looks to how we direct change, not to how we begrudgingly accept the status quo. "The experimental method," Dewey writes, "tries to break down apparent fixities and to induce change."[180]

Just as the empirical method never ends—for we are always testing, trying to improve our understanding, and responding to changing circumstances—democracy is a work-in-progress. Dewey noted that democracy is about "our future conduct" and therefore it "*is an ideal.*"[181] Dewey wouldn't view the charge that his account of democracy is idealistic as troubling at all; he would say that this is precisely the point. As Stuhr nicely puts it:

> [A]s an ideal, democracy is not simply "unreal." As an ideal, it is a deep commitment, grasped by our imagination, that unifies our lives, makes meaningful our efforts, and directs our actions. As an ideal, it is generated through imagination, but it is not "made out of imaginary stuff."[182]

As Stuhr elaborates: "To describe democratic life as an ideal . . . is not so much to state a present fact as it is to recommend a future course of action—and admittedly radical course of action."[183]

The normative goal of democracy for Dewey was a realization of people's full capacities.[184] For Dewey, then, unlike Posner, one cannot simply take human beings and social institutions as one finds them:

> The foundation of democracy is faith in the capacities of human nature; faith in human intelligence, and in the power of pooled and cooperative experience. It is not belief that these things are complete but that if given a show they will grow and be able to generate progressively the knowledge and wisdom needed to guide collective action.[185]

Posner would retort that this vision is too utopian because too many people don't want to participate and aren't educated enough to do anything but vote. Therefore, we should give up on any projects to improve democratic self-government. Dewey's response would be that institutions must be changed; further experimentation is needed in order to structure society so that it becomes more democratic.

For Dewey, democracy cannot take human nature as given. Democracy is about the "maturing and fruition of the potentialities of human nature."[186] Dewey's view of human nature is inspired in part by Darwin, for Dewey recognizes that people constantly adjust and adapt to their environments.[187] Democracy involves the question of developing human potential.

In the end, Dewey was committed to using the power of intelligence to bring about a better society capable of facilitating the growth of individuals. He was convinced that the form and commitment to inquiry that had so decisively enabled us to increase our control over nature in the realm of science and technology might also be used to improve the political governance of society. But he knew that assessment of this claim must wait on the results of trying to put it into practice. From Dewey's point of view, it was far too early to pronounce pragmatic attempts at reconstruction as failures or successes, because by and large they simply had not been tried. This remains true today. Even as Posner recommends our realistic acquiescence to the status quo, his claims that aspirations for a more deliberative society are too utopian seem driven more by his affirmation of the present than by any demonstration that improvement is not possible.

In his recent work, Posner has set out his most thorough account of legal pragmatism to date. It ties a commitment to empiricism with a rejection of philosophical theorizing. In his zeal to attack insular academic philosophical theorizing, however, Posner inexplicably rejects philosophical questioning about our guiding ideals in general. In doing so, Posner's pragmatism departs dramatically from the pragmatic tradition championed by William James and John Dewey. Unfortunately, the consequences of Posner's revisions leave that pragmatic tradition without some of its most useful resources. As we've seen, a study of the development of pragmatism reveals that it has been historically oriented and critical. Pragmatism doesn't reject a role for moral theorizing but recommends instead that we critically reconstruct our normative ideals. The pragmatist tests her ideals in experience. The fact that ideals are not fixed absolutes, but subject to revision and change, doesn't expose the bankruptcy of ideals. It doesn't mean that we should abandon any discussion of ideals or ends, since such ends are essential for guiding our inquiries and practices.

Posner, however, is not interested in promoting methods for the community to develop shared ideals. Rather, the pressing need is for a set of elite managers to serve as efficiency experts whose goal is to find the most efficient means to achieve our inherited ends. Posner's view has significant consequences for thinking about the nature of democratic community. Since people aren't encouraged to make any effort to form a community on the basis of shared ideals, the dominant normative ideals of society are left to drift haphazardly. Society becomes little more than the collective actions of atomistic individuals. Thus, as with the market, Posner views the equilibrium that emerges from individuals who pursue their own private interests as sufficient to generate the larger social ethos.

Posner's pragmatism, having eschewed attempts to critically evaluate ends and having effectively pronounced its agnosticism about community ends, leads naturally to a vision of democracy as principally an efficient mechanism for dispute resolution. This vision of democracy is conservative not only because it privileges the inherited demands of the present, but even more because it rules out as misguided projects of reconstructing community identity through public deliberation. In contrast, the pragmatism of the early pragmatists, especially Dewey, encourages us to approach our present problems more radically. We should subject both means and ends to critical inquiry and empower communities to engage in self-formation by reconstructing the settled habits and ideals that constitute the status quo. For Dewey, "[t]he end of democracy is a radical end. For it is an end that has not been adequately realized in any country at any time. It is radical because it requires great change in existing social institutions, economic, legal and cultural."[188]

Posner is right in his general view that pragmatism has much to offer to law, as well as to democracy. But its contribution is not a rejection of philosophical theory but a transformation of how we relate theory to practice. Far from being banal or timorous, far from accepting our current practices and institutions as given realities, pragmatism subjects them to criticism and reconstruction.

FOUR

Toward a Reconstructive Pragmatism

In defending a pragmatic approach to rights against the charges of Dworkin (for example, that pragmatists ignore precedent), and in seeking to distinguish Dewey's pragmatic reconstruction of values from Posner's abdication of criticism, we also began to consider more general themes of a pragmatist jurisprudence. Building on the work of John Dewey, I argued that like rights, the law itself needs to be understood as a social tool oriented toward the cultivation of conditions conducive to individual growth. In this chapter, I would like to continue to develop that jurisprudence, but in dialogue with less obvious enemies. Many regard Richard Rorty and Stanley Fish as contemporary proponents of a pragmatist philosophy of law. As we shall see, however, they deprive pragmatism of its critical edge and therefore rob jurisprudence of pragmatism's greatest potential contribution, namely, a reconstructive approach to philosophy of law. In place of their deflationary positions, I offer a more Deweyan approach to questions concerning the nature of law, rights, and judicial review.

Richard Rorty famously employed pragmatism to undermine traditional philosophical projects of epistemology. Instead of focusing on our needs for certainty and truth, Rorty encouraged us to focus on the edifying effects of expanding the "conversation of mankind." In his more recent work, he has gone further, suggesting that the focus on justification also shares many of the vices revealed in our obsession with certainty and truth. In light of this, he has recommended shifting focus from inquiry and reconstruction to poetic inspiration. This move comes in concert with increasing interest in developing the connection between law and literature.

It might be thought, in light of Dworkin and Posner, that the pragmatic approach to theory and practice was so radical that it no longer makes sense to consider pragmatism a theory. Rather than look to theoretical engagement as a means for provoking improved practice, perhaps we should seek our inspiration elsewhere—such as in the visions of strong poets. The problem with this approach, which eschews critical reconstruction for redescription, is that it capitulates too quickly when the going gets tough. There's no reason to think that the projects of strong poets, however inspiring they are for projects of private self-creation, can be successful absent work on strengthening communities.

The origin of Dewey's philosophy can be found in the rejection of the conception of philosophy that does not take the situation of philosophical inquiry seriously. Anthony Kronman holds a view of philosophy of the sort Dewey rejects. Kronman, in his 1990 article titled "Precedent and Tradition," claims that genuine philosophy must transcend temporal boundaries and approach problems from a timeless point of view:

> When I am engaged in philosophical thought about a problem in metaphysics or epistemology, I am thinking about the problem from a timeless point of view, from the standpoint, so to speak, of eternity. This point of view is the same tenseless "now" from which Plato and every other philosopher who has ever lived conducted their inquiries as well—at least when they were engaged in philosophy and not the ordinary business of living.[1]

The aim of Dewey's reconstructive critical philosophy could not be more at odds with this view. For Dewey, the problems we encounter are tied up with meanings that have developed over time. When we worry about justice, beauty, and the good, we engage in a dialogue that is rich with historical contributions and provoked by the challenges of contemporary experience.

These problems appear to us the way they do not because they are eternally the same, but because we encounter them in different forms in our day-to-day experience, turning to reflection to help us sort matters out. And not only are the problems mediated through time, but the methods of approaching them are equally time bound. There is no stepping out of the ordinary to some special philosophical realm.

By contrast, Kronman views philosophy as a special discourse that exists outside of the ordinary business of living. When we philosophize, we rise above the details of the ordinary. Dewey insists, on the contrary, that the true test of a philosophy is its very ability to contribute to the improvement of ordinary experience out of which the problems properly arise.[2] One explanation Dewey offers for the entrenchment of views which ignore the practical contributions of philosophy is the suggestion that philosophers of the modern period were forced to cover up their efforts to work toward the improvement of human affairs.

> The heaviest handicap under which philosophy labored in doing this work of liberation was that, instead of doing its work openly, it operated under cover of that which it continued to view as Ultimate Being or Reality at large. Because its work was done under cover, those who engaged in development of the "modern" philosophy of that period mostly failed to note that the service which was genuinely rendered was that of liberation in human affairs.[3]

The persistent resistance to recognizing the contributions of ordinary experience to the formulation and evaluation of philosophical problems lives on as a kind of philosophical hangover from past times. The results, however, serve less to empower "pure" philosophical inquiry and more to hinder efforts to reconstruct the evaluation of philosophical inquiries in such a way that hypotheses can be meaningfully tested.

> Philosophy that is thorough going in acknowledgment that human activities, affairs, successes and failures, trials and tribulations, resources and liabilities, values positive and negative, are its proper subject matter is now able to employ the methods and conclusions of

natural inquiry as its systematic ally in performance of its own office: That of furthering observations of the problems that are deeply and widely involved in the contemporary state of man, and that of contributing to formation of a frame of reference in which pertinent hypotheses for dealing with the problems can be projected.[4]

But even if one recognizes the need to locate the origin of philosophical problems in ordinary experience as a first step, how does one then reconstruct a critical frame of reference that can facilitate such inquiry? This is a question of rationality in a broad sense, of how thinking might gain critical purchase on the practices it would critique.

Many contemporary philosophers have become increasingly disillusioned with the project of establishing a transcendental, universal, atemporal account of reason. The history of this disillusionment can be traced to the late nineteenth century when, with Nietzsche, Freud, and Marx, a deep suspicion regarding the purity of the origins of reason (i.e., its supposed immaculate conception) emerged. It can also be seen in the massive upheaval and transformation of metaphysics occasioned by the American experience and expressed in the words of Peirce, James, Dewey, and Whitehead. It is present in Wittgenstein's attempt to let the fly out of the bottle and rescue the ordinary. We find it in Lyotard's diagnosis of the postmodern condition and his assault on meta-narrative. It takes perhaps its most dramatic form in Rorty's obituary for philosophy and his subsequent turn to the poets for inspiration.

What is the impact of these developments? In postmodern times, we have lost the transcendental measure by which we would rationally order our world and thereby set our own lives in order. The Deweyan critique, amongst others, proceeds by undoing critique in the traditional sense—what it lays bare is not the transcendental conditions of the possibility of critique but, rather, the historical "impossibility" of such conditions. In the face of this collapse of traditional critique, we are left to fill a void. In what follows, I will investigate three candidates for this vacancy: (1) positivist epistemology, (2) Rorty's irony in the context of its relation to the emerging law and literature movement, and (3) Dewey's pragmatic philosophy of reconstruction. I will argue that Deweyan reconstruction has the most to offer contemporary social criticism and philosophy of law.

It is instructive to see how differently the history of philosophy concerning this transition away from belief in transcendental metaphysics is told. Some contemporary analytic philosophers turn it into a story about how logic discloses the contingencies upon which past metaphysical systems have improperly relied in establishing their priority. In this way, reason works itself pure in recognizing and distinguishing the portion of itself that is necessarily true, true in all possible worlds, from the portion of itself, typically considered less important, that is true given the world we live in. In this way, such philosophy liberates itself from the ontological oppressiveness of haphazard contingency; thus, it may focus on working out the necessary conditions of logical thought. Philosophers of this type still expect to find foundational (i.e., necessary) epistemological grounds for rational thinking even if a whole variety of historically accepted transcendental grounds for metaphysics had to be given up.

Such accounts generally produce extremely abstract, minimalist versions of rational method precisely because they sacrifice attention to concrete particularity in order to achieve the maximum scope of application. The more general they become, however, the less useful they are in concrete critical inquiries.

Consider, for example, epistemological debates such as Putnam's with Quine. Putnam argued on behalf of the *a priori* status of some minimal principle of non-contradiction, such as that not every proposition about the world can be both true and false at the same time. If he is right, then we must acknowledge some *a priori* version of this minimal principle of non-contradiction as an operative rule in rational inquiry. In order to ascertain the value of such a contribution, James proposed we submit it to the following pragmatic test:

> Pragmatism . . . asks its usual question. "Grant an idea or belief to be true," it says, "what concrete difference will its being true make in anyone's actual life? How will truth be realized? What experiences will be different from those which would obtain if the belief were false? What, in short, is the truth's cash-value in experiential terms?[5]

It may be, however, that recognition of the kind of rule that follows from Putnam's account is of virtually no practical value at all. This is not to say that it doesn't have significance for epistemological debates, but rather to offer evidence that debates of this sort do little to bolster hope that philosophy can play a meaningful reconstructive role in contemporary legal criticism.[6]

Consider also descriptions of the philosophical project given by philosophers like David Lewis, who have urged us to believe that the only contribution philosophy can make to critical thought is to aid in keeping thinking consistent.[7] Philosophy, in this view, can help us identify whether two propositions are consistent or mutually exclusive. It can also help us determine the extent of our logical commitments upon affirming a particular proposition, but it cannot tell us which propositions to affirm.

> Philosophical theories are never refuted conclusively. . . . The theory survives its refutation—at a price. Perhaps that is something we can settle more or less conclusively. But when all is said and done, and all the tricky arguments and distinctions and counterexamples have been discovered, presumably we will still face the question which prices are worth paying, which theories are on balance credible, which are the unacceptably counterintuitive consequences and which are the acceptably counterintuitive ones. On this question we may still differ.[8]

In other words, philosophy might help us understand the tradeoffs between the civil liberties and civil rights at stake in debates over whether to adopt a campus policy prohibiting "hate speech," but it cannot help us in determining precisely how to strike the balance.[9]

Lewis's view reduces philosophers to consistency police. They provide a sort of external description of the *prima facie* logical tensions between ends, but they are unable to engage in any further discussion of the ranking of such ends qua philosophers. A ranking of this depends, after all, upon historical experience and is not a mere function of the predicate calculus. But this viewpoint ignores just that kind of dialogue between proponents of ends in tension with one another that results in transformation. In other words, the possibility for creative reconstruction amongst competing ends drops out entirely.

Thinkers like Rorty are uncompelled by narrow positivist projects. Unable to find useful work for such philosophies to perform, Rorty gave up talk of rational method. He came to view playful poetic redescriptions proffered by private ironists as more conducive to edification than anything philosophy had to offer: "Literary criticism does for ironists what the search for universal moral principles is supposed to do for metaphysicians."[10] Rorty concludes:

> Ironist philosophy has not done, and will not do much for freedom and equality. But . . . "literature" (in the older and narrower sense), as well as ethnography and journalism, is doing a lot.[11]

In light of accolades such as this, interest in literature as a tool for raising consciousness has been growing. The hope is that literature can inspire individuals to explore their own lives more thoroughly while remaining tolerant of others whose aspirations differ markedly from theirs. In this way, literature can help build a society more amenable to individual expression and self-invention.

Especially striking is the emerging concern with literature evident in law, a discipline that has been traditionally, if not constitutionally, more concerned with cultivating an air of objectivity than an appreciation for fiction. Thus, as legal scholars turn to literature for insight and inspiration, it has become important to ask after the character of this insight and inspiration.

THE TRADITION OF LEGAL REASONING

Recognition of social change is more difficult for some institutions than others. Rate of response, adaptation, and adjustment to such change varies. In this regard, John Dewey singled out legal institutions for special comment.[12] In his view, legal institutions were especially conservative and generally lagged behind other institutions in their responsiveness to the changing facts of our social lives.[13] During the 1930s, when Dewey wrote *Liberalism and Social Action,* this lag was aptly illustrated in the Supreme Court's persistent championing of a conception of laissez-faire liberalism[14] that was out of step with modern industrial production and the webs of mutual interdependence such industrialization created.[15] In present times, our legal institutions are equally slow to come to terms with the need to rethink traditional First Amendment doctrine in light of the problems posed by new forms of communication technologies.[16]

There are structural reasons for the incapacity of our courts to act.

Legal reasoning follows the doctrine of *stare decisis* and gives priority to precedent. Simply put, the fact that a decision on a particular legal issue was made one way by a high court in the past counts itself as a strong reason to decide the issue the same way in the future. In this way, the argument goes, fairness will be served because like cases will be treated in like fashion. Moreover, individuals and corporations will be better able to plan their activities because they will be able to predict how a court will decide a particular case: Courts will decide the legal questions of the future as they have in the past. A virtue of following precedent is that it sounds straightforward, thereby bolstering our confidence that legal rules can be administered fairly. And yet everything depends on how one formulates the not-so-self-evident criteria for determining whether one case is like another. Nonetheless, there is no doubt a genuine measure of comfort for judges in the appeal to objectivity they can lay claim to when basing present decisions upon the precedents of the past.

Unfortunately, many situations contain novel problems unanticipated by the decisions of the past. When the Supreme Court decided in 1957 that obscenity should be judged by "applying contemporary community standards,"[17] they did not envision a world in which daily conversations involving speakers from all over the world would become routine. Which community standards are applicable to an Internet chat room with participants from Paris, Tokyo, and Kansas City? One can somberly intone allegiance to *stare decisis,* but the failure of the past to anticipate the needs of the future cannot be remedied with exhortation. Instead, what is needed is an attempt to think critically about the application of past decisions to new circumstances, along with an attempt to re-vision the future in light of changing social reality. Is "surfing the Net" more like walking in a public square or like shopping at the mall? Will the purposes that were served in the first instance be served again? Or better still, having had time to consider the consequences of the previous decision, was it right? What are the purposes, needs, and worries of speakers in this medium?

Dewey was critical of legal reasoning precisely because of the exaltation of precedent. He worried that such reasoning was all too often a pretense serving to truncate inquiry rather than advance it. In *Art as Experience,* Dewey laments:

Much criticism of the legalistic sort proceeds from sub-conscious self-distrust and a consequent appeal to authority for protection. Perception is obstructed and cut short by memory of an influential rule, and by the substitution of precedent and prestige for direct experience. . . . Judgment which is final, that settles a matter, is more congenial to unregenerate human nature than is the judgment that is a development in thought of a deeply realized perception.[18]

The point is that intense concern with formal justification is no substitute for developing understanding of an issue through investigation. Law as a discipline is preoccupied with justification, but it is all too often justification of a suspect kind. A reader of legal literature, namely law reviews, will notice a related phenomenon: an overwhelming use of footnotes where the function of a footnote is to provide support and justify the propositions asserted in the main text. Almost every assertion, no matter how obvious or banal, is supported by a footnote. If the author asserts that "the sun will come out tomorrow," one can expect a footnote. There is, as Dewey suggests, a kind of distrust of direct experience. An assertion, no matter how obvious, is not grounded unless an authority is cited. There's a corollary: An assertion, no matter how obscure, is grounded if authority is cited. Justification of this kind requires production of citation, but it does not require development of shared understanding.

It is against this background of the priority of precedent and devotion to citation that the increasing attention of legal scholars to literature is most striking. One would not expect, given this characterization of legal reasoning, to find much interest in literature except perhaps as diversion. But in fact there is increasing urgency among some legal scholars to consider what law can learn from literature and how attention to literature might help in attempts to think about legal problems.

EMERGENCE OF LAW AND LITERATURE[19]

The law and literature movement is an umbrella term that covers at least three different activities.[20] There is, perhaps most controversially, the storytelling project. Here, authors such as Patricia Williams have begun to publish first-person narratives in law journals.[21] These narratives seek to explore and relate personal experiences, such as being a black, female law professor at an Ivy League law school. The idea behind these personal narratives is to explore the ways law filters out individual experience and loses the particular before the universal. There is also a plea for empathy in these works, an attempt to simultaneously understand others and to recognize the limits of identification with others.

The second movement is a renewed interest in literature *about* law, in particular such writers as Kafka, Dickens, Camus, and Dostoevsky. Here, the names of Richard Weissberg and James Boyd White come to the fore along with Rorty, who has perhaps been most successful in attracting readers across a spectrum of disciplines.[22] There are many reasons offered for reading fiction, particularly fiction about law, but the primary suggestion is that these authors are in touch with something central in the human condition, something that can be brought back to inform our legal judgment. Rorty puts the point less metaphysically:

> Novels and ethnographies which sensitize one to the pain of those who do not speak our language must do the job which demonstrations of a common human nature were supposed to do. Solidarity has to be constructed out of little pieces rather than found already waiting.[23]

Literature is good for this task of construction, whereas philosophical and legal theory is not.

The third movement is often called "law *as* literature." Here, Fish and others tell us that methods of literary criticism can be applied to law in much the same way they are applied to literature. There is nothing in the texts themselves, be they legal or literary, that resists or requires the application of particular forms of literary critique or analysis.

> Sentences never appear in any but an already contextualized form, and a sentence one hears as ambiguous (for example, "I like her cooking") is simply a sentence for which one is imagining, at the moment of hearing, more than one set of contextual circumstances. Any sentence can be heard in this way, but there are conditions under which such imaginings are not being encouraged.[24]

Fish acknowledges that everything he says about sentences here applies to texts as well. Meaning of the text is regulated not by something internal to the text, but rather by the assumptions of particular interpretive communities (e.g., literary or legal) that engage the text. These communities "look at the objects of the community's concerns with eyes already informed by the community imperatives, urgencies, and goals."[25] Fish calls these assumptions of interpretive communities "background conditions of intelligibility,"[26] and it is these assumptions associated with the particular discourses of law and literature that regulate the range of meanings discovered within the texts subjected to interpretation.

So we can, if we participate in the appropriate community of interpreters, apply the techniques of deconstruction to the reading of a statute just as we can apply them to the reading of a poem. The thought that interpretation is an act of construction is as appropriate in the context of legal writing as it is in any other discourse. And yet the transformative effect of these techniques approaches zero when deployed in a legal context because interpreters, embedded within legal practice, approach their task having already made practice-specific commitments.[27]

Fish insists, therefore, that there is "no benefit to be derived for practice from the pursuit of theory or anti-theory."[28] Or, more cautiously, one might say that Fish renders literary theory safe for legal academics and even judges. True, a literary approach to the law might effect some transformation,[29] but Fish is confident that the aims of the law must always direct and mold the deployment of such techniques to its own purpose. If they do not (i.e., if we accept a thorough deconstructive critique of legal texts), the result would not be an improved law, but the abandonment of law.[30]

LITERATURE AND THE
FUTURE OF RECONSTRUCTION

This increased attention to literature by legal scholars has been prompted in part by hopes that deficiencies in present styles of legal reasoning can be remedied and imaginative thinking about present problems encouraged. Both Rorty and Fish are not enthusiastic, however, about an idea Dewey was very much committed to—that social institutions could be improved and reconstructed through philosophical criticism. Fish, as we have seen, claims that the use of theory or abandonment of it will have no consequences for such institutions, which are, for the most part, driven by contemporary practice and not theory. Rorty, on the other hand, in parting company with traditional metaphysics, believes he must give up the reconstructive ambitions of philosophical critique in his turn to poets for inspiration.

> There is no reason the ironist cannot be a liberal, but she cannot be a "progressive" or "dynamic" liberal in the sense in which liberal metaphysicians sometimes claim to be. She cannot claim that adopting her redescription of yourself or your situation makes you better able to conquer the forces which are marshaled against you.[31]

The literary turn, according to Rorty, involves a recognition of the impotence of philosophical critique along with a newfound appreciation for the power of poets to capture our imagination, broaden acquaintance, and thereby enhance solidarity.

Rorty's rejection of reconstructive ambitions and the consequences of that rejection are manifest in three related ways. First, in accounting for the generation of guiding norms and values, Rorty leaves our education to poets of various strengths. Or, if not to poets, to visionaries who can imagine for us new ways of living together. After citing a passage from Dewey's *Art as Experience,* which emphasizes the importance of imagination for moral progress, Rorty begins to write of "Dewey's Keatsian vision."[32] But one wonders after the origin of such visions. What has informed them historically, and what do they mean given present social circumstance? Perhaps this question is misplaced, however, since Rorty insists that "[v]isions do not really need backup. To put forth a vision is always one of Fitzjames Stephen's leaps in the dark."[33] And yet Rorty seems to confuse "backing-up" metaphysically with investigations into the ways in which existing visions play out in practice and analyses of tensions among rival visions.

Second, Rorty refuses to subject institutional rhetorics to radical critique. He writes, "I think that contemporary liberal society already contains the institutions for its own improvement. . . . Indeed, my hunch is that Western social and political thought may have had the last conceptual revolution it needs. J. S. Mill's suggestion that governments devote themselves to optimizing the balance between leaving people's private lives alone and preventing suffering seems to me pretty much the last word."[34] But it is far from clear what this public/private distinction amounts to and what it would mean to "optimize" it without identifying the priority of various substantive goods. We continue to face the problem of identifying where my nose ends and your fists begin. Moreover, optimism slides into hallucination if one thinks that existing forms of social conversation are models of effective self-critique. The United States has physically outgrown the model of social conversation its democratic vision was predicated upon: the town meeting. It would seem, therefore, that we do need sustained critical and reconstructive reflections on those "institutions" we've established for "our" own improvement.

Finally, inasmuch as Rorty leaves the production of regulative principles to poetic vision and refuses to investigate the institutions wherein these principles are to be applied, his politics leave little room for reconstructive criticism. In fact, he eschews criticism for poetic re-description. In other words, he exchanges criticism for conversion, and revision for new visions. As a result, social change is left to the whims of fashion (i.e., whose vision, which nationality) and relevant power interests.[35] This abandons the heart of the pragmatist project—pursuing programs of reconstructive criticism within practice-specific and institutional settings.

In contrast, Dewey offers an alternative view of the relationship between literature and philosophy. He sees both literature and philosophy as united in the attempt to enhance our perception of present experience, but he also recognizes that they have different tasks.[36] Literature helps us see many perspectives of the world and consider various accounts of the good life, but philosophy concerns itself also with the desirability of the goods presented, the relationships between them, and the methods available for realizing them.

> [The arts of literary discourse] have a freer office to perform—to perpetuate, enhance, and vivify in imagination the natural goods; all things are forgiven to him who succeeds. But philosophic criticism has a stricter task, with a greater measure of responsibility for what lies outside its own products. It has to appraise values by taking cognizance of their causes and consequences.[37]

Reconstructive social criticism must, in Dewey's view, be willing to explore the genetic origin of its guiding principles in terms of narratives, institutions, and what Dewey calls the fabric of experience. One needs to explore the nexus and power relationships among these principles and toward what concrete ends they are directed. Moreover, one must investigate the way existing institutions and practices embody and apply these principles—and how they fail to do so. As one sees one's principles in action—both successes and failures—one works hard to consider, on the one hand, institutions and practices that better embody one's principles and, on the other hand, amendments to principles to make them responsive to new problems.

That literature is important to this visionary project cannot be denied. In particular, within the context of a legal regime wedded to decisions of the past, the ability of literature to facilitate greater depth in constructing our visions for the future should not be ignored. Rorty is right to suggest that novels and poems can provide rich insight into the meanings and values of individuals and cultures foreign to us. However, this insight is only a first step. Often we seek this understanding for a purpose, to help us resolve conflicts or make commitments on behalf of a society. Rorty's injunction to avoid suffering is hardly sufficient guidance in social attempts to reconcile the many, often competing perspectives with which literature acquaints us.

The next step requires thinking about the processes of reconciliation and rectification of the competing goods, interests, and viewpoints that emerge in our inquiry. Dewey gives the name "philosophy" precisely to such attempts.

> Over-specialization and division of interests, occupations and goods create the need for a generalized medium of intercommunication, of mutual criticism through all-around translation from one separated region of experience into another. Thus philosophy as a critical organ becomes in effect a messenger, a liaison officer, marking reciprocally intelligible voices speaking provincial tongues, and thereby enlarging as well as rectifying the meanings with which they are charged.[38]

It is in this sense, as an investigation of multiple discourses, that Dewey understands philosophy as a criticism of criticism, not because it has independent access to the truth by which it would judge other practices, but because it is committed to both enlarging our stock of meanings and rectifying them. This process can also be characterized as reconstruction. The issue, however, is less a matter of preserving the name "philosophy" for this task and more a matter of insisting upon engagements that take seriously both the pluralism of perspectives on the world and the need for organizing them to achieve the best social vision we can.

Although the potential scope of commingled legal and literary investigations is vast—ranging from investigations of the interruptive power of first-person narrative to the elucidation of the human condition—we cannot separate these investigations from the context of inquiry Dewey's work explores. In this context, we must concern ourselves with extensions of ideas (or legal opinions) in practice. Acknowledging the benefits of a turn to literature that ignites the imagination and inspires engagement on behalf of progressive transformation is appropriate. Such a turn, however, does not absolve us of the work of critical social and philosophical inquiry that Dewey championed and Rorty now eschews, but rather it returns us to such work with specific questions and goals in each case, namely, to determine what the literary ideals and characterizations we have encountered would mean if extended into contemporary social practice. Law's turn to literature is promising for reconstructive critique only to the extent that it both opens itself to foreign perspectives and takes up the challenge of judgment and organization necessary to bring better visions into reality.

DEWEYAN RECONSTRUCTION

Dewey rejects both the accounts of rationality proposed by contemporary epistemology and the dismissal of rational critique prefigured in Rorty's turn to the poets. He urges instead the creation of an account of social criticism that, following Hegel, goes beyond discussions of universal structure to engagement with particulars and, therefore, has significance for contemporary models of legal critique. To see why such an account is appropriate in Dewey's pragmatic view, it is important to understand his genealogical account of the origins of thought.

Dewey recognized that describing the character of existence, the traditional province of metaphysics, was not so much dependent upon the taking of epistemological precautions to eliminate incursion of observer interests as it was a matter of becoming increasingly conscious that any description was already a description of the interactive relations of human beings and the world. Put simply, it was the description of human experience; as the primary fact of being in the world, such experience was reducible neither to a subjective nor objective core. Rather, it was constituted precisely in the interactive relationship of what we sometimes call in reflection "subject" and "object" or "human being" and "world."

> "Experience" is "double-barreled" in that it recognizes in its primary integrity no division between act and material, subject and object, but contains them both in an unanalyzed totality. "Thing" and "thought," as James says in the same connection, are single-barreled; they refer to products discriminated by reflection in our primary experience.[39]

For Dewey, therefore, the proper role of metaphysics was to explore and discuss the general traits of this experience as it is found in our day-to-day lives. His view stands up against traditional views of metaphysics that sought to uncover the permanent and stable grounds of reality upon which the seemingly precarious and unstable character of daily existence must ultimately rely. Such metaphysics placed a premium on permanence, whereas Dewey insisted that impermanence and change were no less significant features of experience than permanence and continuity.

In light of this, therefore, it is no surprise that Dewey explained the transition away from transcendental metaphysics in terms of changes in the natural and social circumstances of lived experience. He insisted that we cannot understand developments in logic or law independent from the history of the evolution of the desires and needs of human beings. On the contrary, rational methods themselves, what Dewey called patterns of inquiry, are historically conditioned responses to perceived dissatisfactions.

And yet in saying this, Dewey is not Hegel. One should not read the whole of history as the progressive march of reason. The use of reason, of what Dewey prefers to call intelligence, is simply one aspect of our experience. Moreover, it is an aspect that has only existed for that relatively short stretch of history in which human beings have come to develop their ability to predict, control, and plan future events. The key point to which Dewey would draw our attention is that every employment of human reason is purposive—it presupposes something about the ends for which it is employed.

> Intelligent action is purposive action; if it is a natural occurrence, coming into being under complex but specifiable conditions of or-ganic and social interaction, then purpose like intelligence is within nature, it is a "category" having objective standing and validity.... Purpose is the dominant category of anything truly denominated by history, whether in its enacting or in the writing of it, since action which is distinctively human is marked by intent.[40]

This is why Dewey prefers the term "intelligence," in which he hears the strivings of human beings to use the power of past experience "to shape and transform future experience," as opposed to the terms "rea-son" or "rationality," which have come to have a sterile ring—almost as if they refer to some independent regulatory ideal.[41] One cannot pro-vide an account of intelligent action independently from engaging in a discussion of the purposes toward which that action is directed. Such discussion, moreover, is not simply a matter of mapping logical rela-tionships among ends because an understanding of those ends and their relationships to other ends requires an understanding of the conditions that generated those ends as ends. The projected goals of our inquiry as well as the patterns of inquiry themselves arise within historical experience and function as a response to that experience.[42]

TOWARD RECONSTRUCTIVE LEGAL CRITIQUE

What are the consequences of Dewey's naturalization of metaphysics for future discussions of criticism in general and legal criticism in particular? It suggests that abstract universal accounts of reason pos-ited outside of investigation in particular social practices will, in turn, have little to offer such practices in terms of effective reform. If Dewey is right, our efforts must be redirected toward engagement with vari-ous situated historical institutions and practices, in which social and legal intelligence has arisen and is embodied. Accordingly, in chapter 5, I will provide an example of pragmatic reconstruction with respect to rights and the institution of judicial review.

Making practices more intelligent is not a matter of conforming them to some external rational standard, but rather a matter of critically guiding their development from within to help realize the various ends toward which they strive. Therefore, philosophers should strive, Dewey insists, not to make philosophy more practical but to make practice more intelligent. This requires a shift in focus to various analyses of practices themselves, what Dewey called "reconstruction." This is not an inductive project with the hope of someday having an overarching application, but a constant, directed incrementalism. It does not assert that there is no crossover or interplay of influences among practices; one practice may illuminate another.[43] Instead, it rejects the traditional account of the relation of theory to practice that holds that there is some prior "theory" to be discovered that can profitably be imposed upon practice. In Dewey's view, rationality or intelligence is not something discovered ready-made in theory or in practice; it is something we create in our critical engagement with practices.

As Thomas Grey and others have been careful to point out, it is not as if we will be able to deduce the solution to emerging legal problems via deduction from the first principles of pragmatist theory. He makes this point in the context of explaining that a theory of pragmatism does not provide the solution to problems of harassing speech on campus.[44] Nonetheless, there is perhaps something a little misleading about this claim because it suggests that pragmatism is a kind of free-floating theory, when in fact it is already bound up with a variety of institutions and practices. We don't have to wait for a pragmatic theory in order to begin reconstruction, because the reconstructive effort is already under way in many of Dewey's writings. Take, for instance, Dewey's work on education: Instead of telling us what a theory of rationality looks like in isolation, Dewey begins by trying to flesh out what intelligent action looks like in terms of education and its goals. In his discussion, he appeals to metaphysics at times to give an account of the general structure of experience. This helps us to understand something about what is going on in classroom communication, so there is some sense in which general considerations may be helpful, but not in terms of application of rules. Such general considerations may fund our intuitions so that we go to our discussion of education with certain expectations, but it is primarily in the context of discussion and practice that we discover the most helpful guiding ideals.

For example, Dewey's investigation leads him to recognize that in order to teach someone effectively, you must establish connections with their past and present experience. Moreover, effective education requires matching the means of education to its end. We want to teach citizens how to become able participants in the continual transformation of democratic community and their place in it. This is a very different task from teaching people to memorize their place in society. The memorization strategy works well in feudal societies because, in such societies, that is what one is expected to do: find a vocation and live out one's life. Living in contemporary democratic society, by contrast, requires a different set of skills. There is greater mobility and opportunity for individual choices, so people need to learn how to make decisions in response to that. As a result, education must provide more open-ended decision-making capabilities; emphasizing memorization is not an effective way to do this.

Moving toward a reconstructive theory in law requires a willingness to explore the genetic origins of legal principles, or what Dewey calls the fabric of legal experience. First, one has to ask: Out of what nexus and power relationships did the guiding principles arise, and toward what ends are they directed? Second, one must explore how existing institutions and practices purport to, and fail to, embody and apply these principles. Third, as one studies one's principles in action, both successes and failures, one works hard to imagine more satisfying alternatives.

The cost of not employing a reconstructive model is that either one's principles take the form of pie-in-the-sky platitudes that remain disconnected from concrete practices, or one is forced, as in Rorty's case, to forsake social criticism altogether.

Reconstructing Judicial Review

We began by considering and rejecting a descriptive claim commonly made by communitarians. According to authors such as Glendon and Sandel, contemporary political and legal discourse is dominated and impoverished by concerns over the rights of individuals. As we saw in chapter 1, however, while there is a great deal of talk about rights, case law makes plain that the rights of individuals are often subordinated to community interests. The point is not merely that communitarians have misdescribed present social reality. Rather, in seeking to weaken the status of rights, the communitarians have also weakened the social space wherein individuals can flourish. This is not to say, however, that legal and political theory should retreat into classic liberalism that defends rights as strongholds of negative liberty. Instead, rights must be understood pragmatically, that is as self-conscious, social efforts to foster individual growth. As such, rights are both means and ends.[1] They are means in that they are tools by which a society protects its citizens against unwarranted interference from the state or tyrannical majorities. As a proper result of legislation, rights are also ends to be defended as such.

In defending a pragmatic account of rights against the unsubstantiated charges of Ronald Dworkin (for example, that pragmatists ignore precedent), we also began to consider a more general pragmatist jurisprudence. Building on the work of John Dewey, I argued that like rights, the law itself needs to be understood as a social tool oriented toward the cultivation of conditions conducive to individual growth. In order for this social tool to function properly, it must be supported by critical analyses of the context in which various laws and rights will be enacted. Contra Rorty, therefore, pragmatism cannot do without the kind of critical empirical questions asked by the likes of Dewey. In fact, everything seems to depend on knowing as thoroughly as possible what consequences are likely to follow from particular policy choices. One should not, however, construe such inquiry too narrowly as Posner does. Normative reflections and defenses, for example, in support of rights are integral to the project of jurisprudence.

What has been shown thus far is that a pragmatic approach can avoid many of the objections directed toward it. It can avoid the overly abstract theoretical orientation of Dworkin's jurisprudence without removing critical intent as Posner does or rational content in the manner that Fish and Rorty recommend. A pragmatic philosophy of law is something of a middle path between those overly confident in the authority of principled reasoning and those overly confident in the reconstructive capacity of a historically uninformed imagination. However, an even deeper threat to the cogency of a pragmatic philosophy of law may lie within its own proceedings. In fact, a potentially crippling paradox seems to await any attempt to foster the growth of individuals. A paradox looms here because in attempting to foster the growth of individuals through the institution and revision of laws, pragmatism risks putting the cart before the horse. That is, through paternalistic practices pragmatism risks overdetermining the possibilities open to the very individuals whose autonomy it claims to respect. More precisely, pragmatism risks usurping individual self-creation in favor of a kind of social engineering through the rule of law.

In this chapter, I aim to show that a pragmatic philosophy of law oriented toward fostering individual growth does not fall prey to this paradox. In order to show that this is the case, I will develop what I take to be a pragmatic response to what has come to be known as the "counter-majoritarian difficulty." My point is not that this is a unique problem for pragmatism as opposed to other approaches to jurisprudence. Rather, it is that the counter-majoritarian difficulty contains a problem analogous to the aforementioned paradox. Thus, if one can provide a coherent response to the counter-majoritarian difficulty, then one can also elude the paradox of "engineering" persons capable of self-determination.

The counter-majoritarian difficulty arises because an unelected judiciary exercises the prerogative to void acts of Congress, thus overriding the represented will of the people. This power would seem to render judicial review an inherently anti-democratic practice. The difficulty is analogous to the paradox confronting a pragmatic jurisprudence. Where the courts must justify the seemingly undemocratic manner in which they protect the democratic citizenry against itself, a pragmatic jurisprudence has to account for the initial interpretations of individual growth that it forces upon those very individuals that it claims to protect and empower.

Let's begin by exploring the counter-majoritarian difficulty and imagining a pragmatic rejoinder.

BICKEL'S SCHIZOPHRENIC DEMOCRACY

The counter-majoritarian difficulty enters the philosophy of law through Alexander Bickel's *The Least Dangerous Branch*.[2]

> The root difficulty is that judicial review is a counter-majoritarian force in our system. There are various ways of sliding over this ineluctable reality. . . . The reality that when the Supreme Court declares unconstitutional a legislative act or action of an elected executive, it thwarts the will of representatives of the *actual* people of the here and now; it exercises control, not in behalf of the prevailing majority, but against it. That, without mystic overtones, is what actually happens. . . . It is the reason the charge can be made that judicial review is undemocratic.[3]

According to Bickel, the counter-majoritarian difficulty, with plenty of illicit overtones, continues to haunt contemporary defenders of judicial review. The problem is that having recognized with clarity the "undemocratic" character of judicial review, defenders like Bickel don't want to give it up. On the contrary, Bickel believes that morality requires the government to pursue enduring values,[4] and he believes judicial review fosters this pursuit. That is, he believes the relatively undemocratic Court is more suited to this inquiry than the more democratic, popularly elected political branches.[5] What Bickel wants to know is how to square his desire for a Supreme Court that protects enduring principles against everyday majoritarian politics with his fundamental commitment to democracy.

The first thing to notice about the problem posed in this way is that the counter-majoritarian difficulty is only a difficulty given the account of democracy it presupposes, i.e., majoritarianism. The counter-majoritarian difficulty derives its poignancy precisely because it takes the so-called "actual people," the present majority, as the relevant instantiation of American democratic subjectivity. To frustrate that subjectivity is thereby tantamount to frustrating democracy.

But the mystery of how the Constitution might speak for "the People" need not necessarily lead to a counter-majoritarian difficulty. It is because the Supreme Court is empowered to interpret the Constitution as an expression of the will of the people that one has a counter-majoritarian difficulty. If the majority were so empowered then this specific difficulty would not arise,[6] although one could continue to raise the question whether the majority speaks for "the People" or not (the point is it wouldn't be the "counter-majoritarian difficulty" any longer).

This is worth a moment of reflection. Even if the Constitution were interpreted by the majority, and aside from the questions concerning whether this would vitiate the constitutional goal of checking over-zealous majorities, one might still ask whether majorities are a genuine articulation of the community's will. The worry underlying the counter-majoritarian difficulty is that there is something illegitimate about having platonic guardians in the form of judges impose their will on the whole community. But one can still worry whether there is something illegitimate about having majorities impose their will on other members of the community. Perhaps the only legitimate community decision would be via unanimous vote.[7] This concern is usually handled by political theorists by the insistence that individuals provide their consent, usually tacitly, to the majority decisionmaking procedure of the community. But if this is so, then why does it matter whether it's a majority decisionmaking procedure or not? So what if it's a few of the platonic guardians so long as they obtain each individual's consent?

The point of this digression is simply to show that the counter-majoritarian difficulty is something that is developed alongside an account of democracy that valorizes majorities. But deference to majorities is not itself unproblematic or entirely unmysterious. Is the essential relation of majorities to "the People" one of "speaking for" (a kind of interpretation) or "imposing upon" (an entitlement to impose one's will)? In adopting majoritarian democracy, do majorities "speak for" the community as a whole? Or are they simply entitled via some form of consent to impose their will upon the community as a whole? If the former, then the difficulty at issue is how representation is possible in any event, not simply when a Supreme Court is doing the representing. If the latter, then the issue is whether those being imposed upon can properly be said to have consented to the imposition.

What makes addressing the counter-majoritarian difficulty so complicated is that it is almost impossible to keep these two questions separate. In lieu of laying out complicated strategies for divining the consent (explicit, tacit, hypothetical, or something else) of each and every individual, contemporary discussions have increasingly focused upon the representational function of various institutions. So what becomes important is not the processes by which consent is obtained, such as ratification, but the possibility for authentic representation. Because if the Supreme Court genuinely represents "the People," that is, if it truly re-presents the people just as the people would present themselves, then there is no legitimacy problem whatsoever (assuming that it is in the end a matter of "the People" giving law unto themselves). So we pass over the problem of explicit consent fairly quickly, moving instead to insist that the Supreme Court is empowered (i.e., has consent) to interpret the Constitution but the grant of that power is given upon the condition that in doing so the Supreme Court must represent the will of the people. So with regard to the counter-majoritarian difficulty, the issue of the day becomes how can the Supreme Court truly represent the will of the people? And who are "the People" to be truly represented?

Now, one might begin as Bruce Ackerman does by redescribing our American democratic subjectivity in order to dissolve the tension created by the apparent gap between the wishes of the Supreme Court and the people. But Bickel takes a different route, seeking compensation for tolerating the institution of judicial review that might counterbalance the infringement made manifest by the counter-majoritarian difficulty.[8]

Bickel's position involves tremendous conflict. Although he insists on the "compatibility" of government by consent with a society which respects enduring general values,[9] Bickel spends the largest share of his efforts explaining how we might accommodate the apparent conflict between these goals. Moreover, it seems he has not decided which one is more important. Despite his ever-present affirmations of government by consent, a closer scrutiny suggests ambivalence.

At times, Bickel concedes, in agreement with Lincoln, that principle will have to yield to necessity.[10] And this necessity is often composed of the "prejudices" of the present majorities.[11] "This is nothing to be proud of. It is a disagreeable fact, and it cannot be wished away. It is no service to any worthy objective simply to close one's eyes to it."[12] Such musings appear to reveal both how strongly Bickel values principles while retaining his commitment to subordinating principles to the requirements of democratic government. But the requirements that dominate the landscape at this juncture are not the concerns with legitimacy that undergird the counter-majoritarian difficulty. Bickel isn't worried about the propriety of enforcing upon the majority the principle that demands abolition of slavery. Instead, he is worried about whether the majority will put up with such an imposition. Look at the language:

> The hard fact of an existing evil institution such as slavery and the hard practical difficulties that stood in the way of its sudden abolition justified myriad compromises short of abandoning the goal. The goal itself—the principle—made sense only as an absolute and as such it was to be maintained. . . . But expedient compromises remained necessary also, *chiefly* because a radically principled solution would collide with widespread prejudices, which no government resting on consent could disregard, any more than it could sacrifice its goals to them.[13]

There are many points of interest. First, the central reason for not implementing the principled solution appears to be the risk of social upheaval.[14] Second, the worthy goals alluded to (the enduring values?) must, apparently, be derived from a source other than the inclinations of present majorities, here characterized as mere "prejudice."[15] Given the priority of these concerns, it seems silly to give the counter-majoritarian difficulty center stage. The vexing problem here is not the counter-majoritarian difficulty but incorporation of the good without reactionary regression or the horrors of revolt. The point seems less a concern with why judicial elites are justified in thwarting the will of the actual people and more a concern with how much they can get away with in directing social transformation toward the good without incurring practical setbacks.

Of course, Bickel might respond that it turns out coincidentally that the Court is justified in thwarting the will of the actual people, as determined by some independent analysis, precisely at that point where practical setbacks would arise. Or, more plausibly, he might respond that the practical setbacks simply occur at that point where the will of the people is illegitimately thwarted. This would be a good response but it is not consonant with his general analysis. The analysis sets the baseline criteria for legitimacy in accordance with the majoritarian democracy model presupposed by the counter-majoritarian difficulty. But we are far removed from that already with any application of judicial principle that runs counter to majority preferences, no matter how tempered the application. Since Bickel endorses such applications, recognizing that they can often be pursued without incurring on-balance counter-productive setbacks, it is clear there is an acceptable range of judicial action which thwarts the will of the actual people. Of course, he may still insist that what finally makes judicial action unacceptable is the intensity with which it frustrates the will of the people and not the practical difficulties that ensue at that juncture. If so, then we should really wonder why Bickel would have us take the counter-majoritarian difficulty so seriously in the first place. Why not just say that short of this kind of intensity of frustration there is no serious problem in frustrating the will of the actual people and the baseline presupposed by the counter-majoritarian difficulty is of little import?

This would seem to follow from his own concluding recommendations for the Court, namely to endorse only those principles which will in time, preferably the short run, "gain general assent."[16]

> The Court is a leader of opinion, not a mere register of it, but it must lead opinion, not merely impose its own; and—the short of it is—it labors under the obligation to succeed.[17]

Here Bickel makes the Court accountable at the time of their decision not to the *actual* people as suggested by the formulation of the counter-majoritarian difficulty, but rather to some imagined future people. He thereby frees the Court from its democratic commitments to the actual people that are so important to the poignancy of the counter-majoritarian difficulty in order to give them space to pursue principle. His guiding injunction could be stated as follows: pursue principle within the bounds of practicality (i.e., recognize both the potential for and limit to the transformational possibilities of the people).

Recall that Bickel's principal worry with regard to the counter-majoritarian difficulty concerned thwarting the will of the people here and now in favor of a mystical will hovering somewhere between the Court and the citizenry. Unfortunately, Bickel's solution to the counter-majoritarian difficulty trades on an all-too-mystical and abstract presumption about the will of future people. Bickel therefore does not confront the counter-majoritarian difficulty; instead, he avoids and buries it.

ACKERMAN'S TRIP TO DELPHI: KNOW THYSELF

Ackerman does not take Bickel's simplistic account of the counter-majoritarian difficulty seriously, that is, he does not believe that the difficulty revolves around the inability of the Court to act in accordance with the wishes of the present majority. On Ackerman's view, the American democratic subject is constituted not only by present majorities but also by past decisions and debates.

The term "American democratic subjectivity" is mine, and not Ackerman's, but by employing it I can capture the key difference between Ackerman's approach to the counter-majoritarian difficulty and Bickel's approach. Bickel assumes that democratic legitimacy turns on representing present majorities, whereas Ackerman realizes that what needs to be represented is a somewhat thicker embodiment of the democratic spirit initiated by the Constitution but transformed through history. It is never just present majorities that are important, however, because our present is historical and it can claim to have self-knowledge only through study of the past.

Ackerman argues for what he calls "dualist democracy." This democracy is composed of two key political moments: normal politics and abnormal politics. In moments of normal politics, average citizens go on about their lives concerned primarily with their private aims while leaving the administration of government to elected and appointed officials. In moments of abnormal politics, in contradistinction, citizens mobilize and assert their rightful claim to determine the future of our constitutional democracy.

> Above all else, a dualist Constitution seeks to distinguish between two different decisions that may be made in a democracy. The first is a decision by the American people; the second, by their government.
>
> Decisions by the People occur rarely, and under special constitutional conditions. Before gaining the authority to make supreme law in the name of the People, a movement's political partisans must, first, convince an extraordinary number of their fellow citizens to take their proposed initiative with a seriousness that they do not normally accord to politics; second, they must allow their opponents a fair opportunity to organize their own forces; third, they must convince a majority of their fellow Americans to support their initiative as its merits are discussed, time and again, in the deliberative fora provided for 'higher lawmaking.' It is only then that a political movement earns the enhanced legitimacy the dualist Constitution accords to decisions made by the People.[18]

Of course, given this account it becomes very important to determine what the conditions are for recognizing the transition from normal to abnormal politics. Ackerman claims that when one party wins four general elections in a row, that suggests they have mobilized the people on behalf of their political vision.[19]

So the issue of legitimacy underlying the counter-majoritarian difficulty is not simply whether a policy or decision thwarts the will of present majorities but whether it undercuts our American democratic subjectivity more generally. To determine this, the Court is employed and insulated not so that it can rule on the good, but so it can show the American people to themselves in a more historical way.

The Court is privileged to do this within the scheme of government established at a moment of abnormal politics, a scheme that can be changed in yet another such moment. Why is it so privileged? It is not a matter of thwarting the will of the people because principle is more important than that will, but rather a matter of helping the American people understand their own self-constitution because principle is so very important to that constitution.

Ackerman's community subject undercuts the counter-majoritarian difficulty before it gets started. It stretches back to include in its subjectivity the last moments of abnormal politics and thereby is rendered autonomous. It gives voice to the grandeur that is lacking in our normal politics, and yet it is difficult to believe that these democracy-making powers reside in us (our better half?). The problem is, it is questionable whether "we" ever get to experience our wondrous autonomy. We might not even recognize the point at which we enter into a moment of abnormal politics, particularly if such a moment contains neither an amendment nor constitutional convention.

The experience of unfreedom in normal politics is offset by the acknowledged free play of our larger community subjectivity. It continues expressing itself through those constitutional mechanisms created or reaffirmed during the last moment of abnormal politics. Hence, the counter-majoritarian difficulty is dissolved because the responsibility of American democracy is to itself (a complex subjectivity) and not merely to present majorities, but the participatory moment that constitutes itself is the last moment of abnormal politics, and the contribution of present selves in moments of normal politics looks marginal at best.

So the question becomes, why endorse such a view? One set of answers revolves around how well such a view accounts for our present system. And this turns, in part, on what one thinks the Constitution is supposed to do. Should it enable us to be privatists for the most part, that is citizens who allow government to guide civic affairs except for rare moments of mobilization, or should it enable us to participate in the construction of the public good more regularly? Ironically, although Publius[20] exalts the public-regarding over the private-regarding, the system he endorses makes private citizenship largely an exercise in frustration. Indeed, it liberates individuals to concern themselves chiefly with private-regarding issues without worry that the deeper structures of American democratic subjectivity will be altered while they aren't paying attention, but it also thereby encourages individuals not to pay attention because such attention is unlikely to amount to any deep-seated change.[21]

On the other hand, it's not really true that present citizens are confined to normal politics, because it is up to these same present citizens (in their various private and public capacities) to interpret American democratic subjectivity. So it turns out that the state of affairs which issued from the last moment of abnormal politics (i.e., present normal politics), conditions the understanding of that last moment. We, present selves, participate in construing the American democratic subjectivity that forms us. Of course, the Supreme Court is the institution that in the end gets to construe American democratic subjectivity, but its construction is not unrelated to the various goings on in society at large. Hence, ironically, the community subject which sets us free may be largely the product of the normal politics it was meant to regulate.

The point is not that we can construe American democratic subjectivity any way we like from normal politics. Indeed, our present constitution involves the historical internalization of American democratic subjectivity. The point is that there is no escaping the difficult hermeneutic work surrounding our self-identity. The point of access to the inquiry concerning American democratic subjectivity, and the last moment of abnormal politics that produced the present determination of American democratic subjectivity, is the present state of normal politics, itself formed from previous constitutional determinations. "We" are left, therefore, continually working out the question of our own self-constituting and becoming. So Ackerman's insistence on dualism pays critical dividends, not because it dissolves the counter-majoritarian difficulty and the angst accompanying it,[22] but because the tension it creates doesn't allow platitudinal gestures toward "majorities" to stand in for more complex analyses of American democratic subjectivity. At times, dualism seems to project the animating autonomy of American democratic subjectivity wholly into a largely inaccessible moment of abnormal politics with equally platitudinal promises of the possibility of mobilization. And yet, upon closer inspection, the conditions for mobilization (or alternatively, for satisfying the rules of recognition for abnormal politics) are achieved by individuals in normal politics, individuals who articulate self-consciously a sustained account of their social identity counter to prevailing historical narrative. So individuals in normal politics are empowered as agents of historical transformation, but the exercise of that agency (satisfying the rules of recognition) demands attention to its own historical formation.

THE PROCEDURAL ALTERNATIVE OF
JOHN HART ELY

One could say that the ratifying of the Constitution was a contract in which all participants consented to allowing the Supreme Court to undertake judicial review. The Court does its job by interpreting the Constitution. This is an Elyesque interpretivist position.[23] The Supreme Court is empowered to interpret the Constitution and is free to do so within the interpretive leeway it is given. But on this view, where does there arise any responsibility to the present majority? Ely takes such a responsibility to be central in sketching his representation-reinforcing paradigm for understanding the legitimacy of judicial review, but is it? The heart of his argument is that the Constitution is about achieving the best form of representation possible and this means, at times, regulating the whims of present majorities so that they will represent better. One has a kind of institutional competence argument at work: the Constitution is dedicated to representation, and while primarily majoritarian institutions serve those ends better, there are times when the Supreme Court does. So frustrating the will of present majorities is a problem because of our general intuition that the majorities best represent the community. Thus, the counter-majoritarian difficulty is a real problem. However, when it can be shown that majorities would hinder rather than help foster democratic representation, then we need not be embarrassed to turn to the Court.[24]

In Ely, what seems to be emerging is a middle way of responding to the counter-majoritarian difficulty between the stark choices of consent to a system of government in which judges make constitutional decisions and a system of government where judges are empowered to speak for "the People." This is the representational-reinforcing strategy; one goes one step backward to go forwards. Initially, you recognize that what underlies the counter-majoritarian difficulty is a concern with legitimacy understood primarily in terms of representation. Then one moves forward by making a commitment to representation understood as a procedural ideal that enables the regulation of majorities. It is legitimate to do so, because that representational ideal, although embodied in majorities and the reason we find the counter-majoritarian difficulty problematic, is more basic and distinguishable.

Thus, in turning to the question of how one squares the practice of judicial review with a commitment to democracy, there appear to be three strategies. First, one can try to maintain the legitimacy of the judicial decision by redescribing community subjectivity so that it is not simply reducible to present majorities, and then explain how judicial review properly responds to the will of that subjectivity. Second, one can go one step back and say that underlying the legitimacy claim is a commitment to representation, a kind of regulative ideal one can properly impose upon present majorities because it's the same ideal present majorities draw their sustenance from. Third, one can simply argue that although judicial review ignores the will of present majorities, it is a good institution for articulating principles that will serve the furtherance of the community.

Ackerman uses the first strategy, Ely the second, and Bickel, in a problematic way, both the first and third. The great amount of attention dedicated to this problem suggests that the counter-majoritarian difficulty is as central as Bickel claimed. He also claimed that it is mysterious to solve the problem by redescribing the community subjectivity so that "the People" does not refer to the present majority. And yet he himself does so, although he employs other strategies as well. So although Bickel may be right that appeals to "the People" are mysterious, and he may be right that we need to take the counter-majoritarian difficulty seriously, it does not follow that there is a response to our counter-majoritarian concerns that is not at some level mysterious. To investigate this, one needs to investigate the responses.

I claimed above that there seemed to be only two alternatives for legitimacy (delegation or representation), but here I catalog three responses. How so? The problem is Ely's middle way. It appears coherent as an independent option but closer scrutiny will show that it is not. Even if one says that the concern underlying our commitment to majoritarian democracy is a concern with achieving the best representation, the question instantly arises: representation of what? The answer can't simply be the majority because then it's impossible to figure out how this underlying principle could be used to regulate the majority. And with the emergence of the question of what is to be represented, one is thrown into the problem of describing (unmysteriously) the community subject. Of course, Ely could argue that the Court somehow represents majority interests better than the majority does itself, given the nature of the respective political institutions available to do this. But this would confound central tenets in his text. The more plausible move would be to say that at some time, perhaps at the founding, the Court was chosen by a strong majority to decide issues of constitutional principle and it is representative, not in saying what those people would say, but in being chosen to speak on certain constitutional issues. This might explain why it's acceptable for the Court, understanding itself as bound to a decision of past generations, to make constitutional decisions and frustrate present majorities, but it still leaves undefended the proposition that present majorities should be bound by the ideas of past generations.

Note that the reason previous generations may have delegated such decisions to the Court might be understood in terms of the third strategy discussed, the compensation strategy. Judicial review is chosen, and is acceptable, because it has institutional advantages for ascertaining and promulgating principles important to the maintenance of a democratic community. Or one might simply use the third strategy to argue that certain principles outweigh majority preferences. The key question remains: Is the legitimacy of judicial review a function of its being chosen in some way, or a function of the credibility of the principles it endorses. The middle way has evaporated.

So Bickel is right that there is no evading substantive debate. Unfortunately, his account of where that debate occurs, in a realm other to the constitution of American subjectivity presupposed by the counter-majoritarian difficulty, leaves the relation of substantive principles to the subjectivity of the American democratic process insufficiently explored. And as a result, his work harbors a schizoid account of democracy that ultimately tears it apart. Ely realizes that the question of American self-constitution is at the fore, but he mistakenly thinks he has all the substantive guidance he needs once he assumes the majoritarian intuitions underlying the counter-majoritarian difficulty. Unfortunately, once one admits that translating those intuitions into political practice is not self-evident and requires the deployment of regulative ideals, then one needs an account of those regulative ideals. This involves substantive debate over the appropriate principles for guiding such translations, and there is no way to avoid it.

So, although Bickel is right that appeals to "the People" as a whole are mysterious, they also seem to be unavoidable. The point is we need to say something more to justify such appeals, but that's not a unique weakness. Majoritarian decisionmaking must be justified too, else one might expect the requirement of unanimity. Moreover, the fact that appeals to "the People" other than present majorities of the here and now is mysterious doesn't stop Bickel from employing them. Indeed, he employs both the first and third strategies. He makes the decisions of the judiciary responsible to "the People" of the future. He recommends that the Court only endorse those principles which will in time, preferably in the short run, "gain general assent."[25] Thus, in the re-description of "the People" one gets either an elimination of the mystifying element (ah, I see, "the People" include their future selves) or more mystification (huh? "the People" are who-they-are-not-yet?). But Bickel also puts endorsement of absolute principles[26] before adherence to majority will in many instances. So Bickel tries two separate ways, at times in tension with each other, to alleviate the pressure of the counter-majoritarian difficulty. But in doing so, because he is unwilling to completely endorse the compensation strategy, he remains saddled with the problem of appropriately characterizing "the People" without "mysteriously" referring to a community subjectivity that is richer than present majorities. And he can't solve it.

But one shouldn't conclude from all this that mystification is not a real worry. The fact that there's no escaping arguments about what American democratic subjectivity consists in by simple appeal to majorities or otherwise does not mean that some of those arguments are better and less mystifying than others. If one accepts Ackerman's account, then the empirical subject is wowed with tales of its world-making powers at moments of abnormal politics. And yet the tale is generally told precisely to those empirical subjects that aren't participating in that way. Sure, the promise of mobilization is held out, but the barriers to entry are so high it doesn't seem unreasonable to be dubious of the claim: "Come the Mobilization, you, as part of the community subject, will be free in your action." The cost of including oneself in the political and historical narrative might be read as an act of tremendous debasement, just the kind of thing Bickel worries about when he talks about mystification. The worry is that we get the Constitution speaking for "the People" precisely by ignoring the present people. Bickel's exhortation to the Court to consider the future selves of the people might seem equally damning, but is it? It seems impossible to project future selves without tremendous attention to present selves. But Ackerman believes we can look at what past individuals thought without confusing it too much with what present individuals think. So the likelihood of arriving at precisely the position Bickel feared, where we are telling dissatisfied present selves to affirm the status quo or achieve an amazing mobilization, appears great. It's reasonable to wonder how justified it would be to hold the present community to decisions made by a past community simply because they can't get an amendment through or sustain eight years of party-line politics.

Nonetheless, Ackerman's position provides insight into how a pragmatist jurist concerned with developing conditions conducive to individual growth can escape the paradox of determining the possibilities open to the very individuals whose autonomy it seeks to establish and further. Ackerman's position implies that we should not think of the present majorities as the appropriate instantiation of our American democratic subjectivity. Our American democratic subjectivity is thicker than this. Hence, if one wants to debate on Ackerman's terms about who we are, one must confront dominant narratives and histories with counter-narratives and genealogies. This is essentially what the Court does when it offers an account of how the Constitution will be read to meet changing social conditions. The Court doesn't possess a special illocutionary force that makes its reading so simply in virtue of the Court's pronouncing it. Rather, the Court presents a particular account of our American democratic subjectivity to the populace and says "this is who we've become."

In response, if the people aren't happy with who they've become, they can instigate a counter-movement to challenge the Court's account or remake themselves. This possibility for effective response is crucial. When a pragmatist jurist argues for stronger speech rights as a condition conducive to individual growth, she must offer a genetic account. A pragmatist does not simply embrace individualism as an abstract first principle, but rather claims that our American democratic subjectivity has been interested in individuals and their growth. Her claim is that changes in the structure of the community warrant rethinking the role of rights.

For example, one might consider how the space for exercise of classic individual rights has been delimited by the growth of managerial contexts as made clear in Robert Post's analysis.[27] The pragmatist proposes a response, but in doing so recognizes her location in the present historical moment and sees her efforts as part of a community conversation that has historical depth. She isn't in a paradoxical position because she isn't saying simply that her account of individualism should be enacted, but rather is making that claim within the context of a public discussion.

Ackerman's account is interesting precisely because it helps us realize that the Court is relating not only to the present, but relating to American democratic subjectivity. Hence, the Court is reflecting back to a given present community who that community has become and allowing that community to act to reject the Court's description. In similar fashion, a pragmatist philosophy of law is not making law, but rather asking how we should view ourselves and the laws that govern us. It understands itself as a kind of practice that tries to stimulate the kind of self-reflection that the Ackerman jurist can, and it confronts the public with an account of American democratic subjectivity. The pragmatist does not say to the community: "We are going to manufacture this kind of individual and you will appreciate it," because she recognizes that those very individuals in the public conversation to which pragmatic jurisprudence belongs can respond and challenge the account presented.

For example, consider my challenge to communitarians' claims that they've misread the message of important Supreme Court decisions concerning individual rights. They can respond with competing redescriptions. It is true that I begin as a committed pragmatist, but there is no paradox where I must establish conditions to produce the very individuals who need to be there in order to accept and deliberate over the conditions I am trying to establish. Rather, I address individuals already on the basis of an understanding of American democratic subjectivity. And although I'm offering a genealogical account of this understanding of who we are and who we're becoming and suggesting this should inform who we should become, the vitality of this account depends upon affirmation or rejection from the community to which it is addressed.

SIX

Pragmatism, Genealogy, and Democracy

A pragmatic approach to philosophy of law is one that understands itself as part and parcel of existing political conversations about the nature and ends of the polis. Whereas Dewey would talk about "the public and its problems," I have suggested, given a pragmatic reading of Ackerman, that one should view the addressee of much contemporary legal theory in terms of what I call American democratic subjectivity.

As we saw in chapter 5, a more nuanced understanding of our American democratic subjectivity provides an escape to the counter-majoritarian difficulty classically conceived. It denies what the counter-majoritarian difficulty presupposes, namely that remaining true to democracy is simply a matter of remaining faithful to majorities. Rather, our American democratic subjectivity embodies the aims of citizens expressed across a historically extended period. It understands the population of democratic citizens not with reference to a count of citizens at a single point in time, but with reference to how that population has expressed itself through popular votes and the actions of its representatives and institutions across a significant stretch of time.

The import of this analysis, however, is not simply that it avoids the counter-majoritarian difficulty and the related problems of paternalism in a pragmatic defense of rights. More importantly, it underscores how legal philosophy participates in democratic decisionmaking writ large. Dewey writes in *The Public and Its Problems:*

> The strongest point to be made in behalf of even such rudimentary political forms as democracy has already attained, popular voting, majority rule and so on, is that to some extent they involve a consultation and discussion which uncover social needs and troubles.[1]

Through its genealogical expositions of American democratic subjectivity, a pragmatist philosophy of law renders explicit social needs and the various legal remedies designed to meet them, thereby enabling the democratic public to systematically confront and reflect upon who it has become through the recent past. Such practices of social memory are not merely nostalgic, however. Rather they enable the democratic public to self-consciously decide whether or not to continue with its prevailing trajectory or whether a new course of action is required.

Just because a pragmatic philosophy of law facilitates public inquiry and debate, one should not think that it remains disinterested. Its genealogies always proceed with an eye oriented toward realizing particular futures, thus closing the gap between legal theory and practice that so often plagues the philosophy of law. Pragmatist arguments about legal theory are forms of practice that participate within the larger dialogue about our present American democratic subjectivity.

Historically self-conscious and politically engaged, the pragmatist insists that legal theory needs to understand itself as a participant in democratic dialogue about who we have been, who we are, and who we should become. On the one hand, the legal pragmatist does not make authoritative announcements concerning her vision of the good life, then seek to enforce that account through legislation. On the contrary, she understands herself as trying to empower intelligent decisionmaking within the present community by rendering the legal past explicit while laying out possible futures. In contrast to Kronman's account of philosophizing as his engagement with the eternal, when the pragmatist thinks about what she is doing as a legal philosopher, she recognizes that she is participating in dialogue about how we should deploy legal concepts in the context of our American democratic subjectivity. She realizes her activity is part and parcel of a democratic process and not outside of it. She can contribute to that process by offering a richer understanding of the present democracy to the interlocutors and by helping facilitate intelligent formation of the community will.

Viewed generally then, this book has been concerned with developing a pragmatic orientation to law in general. For the pragmatist, however, general orientations are always informed by particular engagements. I attempted to exemplify this reflective approach to inquiry in chapter 1 by intervening in the current communitarian debate over rights. If one looks at that engagement, one can see why it is pragmatic. First, it responds to existing conversations and the needs of the present that emerge therein. It does not begin with an inquiry into the nature of rights *per se* in order to deduce the policies that should follow logically from that concept. Instead, my inquiry commenced with a look at the role of individual rights in contemporary society.

Second, I argued that an analysis of our present situation suggests the need for stronger rights to protect a sphere for individual expression against the increasing pressures exerted by an ever-expanding bureaucratic and administrative environment. Contrary to the communitarians, therefore, it is not that rights talk has corrupted public discourse but that existing institutions have undermined the ability of individuals to reflect upon and render meaningful decisions concerning their own lives. I regard my intervention in this debate as an instance of what Dewey called criticism of criticism, that is, a criticism of reigning presumptions and ends concerning a sphere of practical concern. I call this pragmatic because my analysis focuses upon the worth of the communitarian critique in light of its ability to accurately read our political present and realize the aspirations embodied in our democratic subjectivity.

Looking back on chapter 1, one can see that the rights discussion is an instance of the kind of inquiry that pragmatists should pursue. It is still true that the pragmatic injunction to remember that all thought occurs in a context shot through with needs, purpose, and desire remains useful. It performs a useful service in dissuading theorists from talking as if there were transcendental ideals that could regulate our practices without being influenced by the very practices it must regulate. Nonetheless, after a time, we need to move beyond simply cautioning concern for context in general to attempts to specify our present context and engage the problems that emerge therein. I take my discussion of rights to have initiated such a move.

Besides offering a general orientation for a pragmatic philosophy of law, and beyond embodying that orientation through a particular discussion of rights, I have also attempted to address existing and potential criticisms of a pragmatic approach to philosophy of law, and with some surprising consequences.

Ronald Dworkin thinks it is precisely around a defense of rights that a pragmatist would not have anything cogent to say. However, as we saw in chapters 1 and 2, Dworkin's attack depends on his mischaracterization of the pragmatic position on two counts. First, he suggests that the pragmatic judge would be all too ready to abandon precedent on behalf of a better future, thus imperiling the realization of fairness and predictability. But pragmatic method, properly applied, yields no principled objection to furthering these goals. Moreover, as we saw in chapter 5, a pragmatist philosophy of law only comes into its own when it adopts a genealogical perspective on past decisions and American democratic subjectivity in general.

As one can see, therefore, Dworkin's claim that pragmatists are unconcerned with history is surprisingly off the mark. In fact, pragmatic theories of valuation explicitly recognize their dependence on historical reflection in securing the realization of values in the changing circumstances of the present. Pragmatists differ from Dworkin in that they do not reify past experience in terms of authoritative precedent.

Posner, despite issuing an appropriate challenge to Dworkin, provides a defense of pragmatism that seeks to appeal to "common sense" but is considerably off target upon reflection. He views ideals as useless and philosophical theorizing as empty. Since, on his view, there is no way to effectively scrutinize social goals, pragmatism devolves into little more than an efficiency exercise. The task of the pragmatist becomes merely finding the appropriate means to achieve our given ends. Upon closer inspection, however, it is precisely the concern with criticizing ends that motivates the classical pragmatic inquiry into experience.

Perhaps even more surprising is the distance that separates the pragmatic approach to philosophy of law envisioned here from the neo-pragmatisms of Richard Rorty and Stanley Fish. While many now equate pragmatism with their deflationary approaches to abstract theoretical concerns, we have seen that one must not lose sight of empirical questions concerning present social situations when contextualizing the meaning of central theoretical concepts like "rights." Contra Rorty, therefore, poetry and imaginative redescription, no matter how strong or novel, is no substitute for the kind of concrete social inquiry that Dewey's work on education and individualism exemplifies. Surprisingly, pragmatism is a true protector of imagination insofar as it concerns itself with considering concretely the conditions necessary for realizing particular social visions and the consequences that will follow.

It is amazing that although many people assume they know what a pragmatic philosophy of law would consist in, one finds so many surprises upon closer inspection. It is surprising that Rorty and Fish consider pragmatic approaches which give up reconstructive ambitions. In light of Dworkin's critique, it is surprising to discover that pragmatists really are deeply concerned with the past. Moreover, after Posner, one might expect pragmatists to have no interest in a concept as abstract as rights. Yet, given a concern with the lack of conditions for individual flourishing in the present, there are strong pragmatic reasons for reconsidering the role of rights.

In a way this should all not be so surprising. Pragmatism must always surprise itself because it seeks to respond to the present. Because ends are always in the process of becoming new means, because the demands of the present are always shifting, pragmatism can never rest. It is not, after all, a precast *a priori* position. Instead, as the committed application of critical intelligence to live problems, it must re-invent itself even as it reflects upon its past, and more importantly our past, in order to secure a richer future.

NOTES

INTRODUCTION

1. See "The Revival of Pragmatism," 18 Cardozo L. Rev. (1996), 1; "The Renaissance of Pragmatism in American Legal Thought," 63 S. Cal. L. Rev. (1990), 1569.

2. Thomas C. Grey, "Holmes and Legal Pragmatism," 41 Stan. L. Rev. (1989), 787, 814. See "The Revival of Pragmatism"; "The Renaissance of Pragmatism in American Legal Thought."

3. See Richard Rorty, "The Banality of Pragmatism and the Poetry of Justice," in *Pragmatism in Law and Society*, ed. Michael Brint & William Weaver (Boulder, Colo.: Westview, 1991) ("I think it is true that by now pragmatism is banal in its application to law.").

4. Thomas Grey, "Hear the Other Side: Wallace Stevens and Pragmatist Legal Theory," 63 S. Cal. L. Rev. (1990), 1569, 1590; see also Rorty, "The Banality of Pragmatism and the Poetry of Justice," 89 (quoting Grey).

5. Rorty, "The Banality of Pragmatism and the Poetry of Justice," 90.

6. A study undertaken by Fred Shapiro, Associate Librarian for Public Services at Yale Law School, has discovered that Posner is the most cited contemporary author of non-treatise legal books and articles. Posner had 7,981 citations, while the next most cited author, Ronald Dworkin, had 4,488. Am. Law, Dec. 1999, 107.

7. Richard Posner, *Law, Pragmatism and Democracy* (Cambridge, Mass.: Harvard University Press, 2003).

8. Ibid., 73.

1. WHAT'S RIGHT WITH RIGHTS AND WRONG WITH COMMUNITARIANISM?

Erin Wiser, as quoted in *Los Angeles Times*, 22 February 1996, A1.

1. A similar fate followed for extracurricular clubs in the Orange Unified School District in Orange County, California: "Now, faced with a lawsuit and a judge's preliminary injunction, the district is considering a new approach: whether to vote on Thursday to ban all 38 non-curricular clubs, including the Black Student Union and the Gentlemen's Club, as a way of halting the gay group's meetings. Only one other school district, Salt Lake City, has taken such

an approach, and a lawsuit against that district is still moving through the courts." *New York Times*, 10 February 2000, A20. The result of the vote was to eliminate extracurricular clubs at elementary and middle schools and to modify the rules for participation in high school clubs to require parental consent and a minimum 2.0 grade point average. Clubs will also be required to avoid discussions of a sexual nature. See *New York Times*, 12 February 2000, A8.

2. See *Lamb's Chapel v. Moriches Union Free Sch. Dist.*, 508 U.S. 384 (1993). In this unanimous decision written by Justice White, the Court evaluated a school board decision to deny the use of school facilities to an evangelical group that wished to show a six-part film series concerning child-rearing and family issues advocating a pro-Christian point of view. The school board's decision was rendered pursuant to their interpretation of a New York state law that expressly permitted after-hours use of school property for social, civic, and recreational activities but did not mention religious activities. The Lamb's Chapel petitioners claimed that although the school board need not have opened their classrooms for any form of after-hours use, the fact that they did open their classrooms for social and civil purposes meant "that restrictions on communicative uses of the property were subject to the same constitutional limitations as restrictions in traditional public forums such as parks and sidewalks" (White, 508 U.S. 391). The Court refused to rule on this issue, though it noted the petitioner's argument had "considerable force." Instead, the Court concluded that the petitioners were denied access to the school because of their religious views. It wasn't the topics of child-rearing and family issues that were excluded, but rather a particular approach to those topics. Such viewpoint discrimination is unconstitutional: "The principle that has emerged from our cases 'is that the First Amendment forbids the government to regulate speech in ways that favor some viewpoints or ideas at the expense of others' " (White, 508 U.S. 394, quoting *City Council of Los Angeles v. Taxpayers for Vincent*, 466 U.S. 789). In choosing to ban all extracurricular activities, the Salt Lake City Board of Education was hoping to avoid two challenges to its ability to exclude the gay clubs. First, it wanted to avoid having the school facilities accorded the same constitutional protections as traditional public forums, in which case the board would need a compelling state interest to justify regulation of speech beyond time, place, and manner restrictions. Second, it wanted to avoid the challenge of viewpoint discrimination. It is not permissible to regulate speech in a way that favors one viewpoint over the other, which any law excluding only the gay clubs would appear to do. Accordingly, the board decided to implement an across-the-board ban of extracurricular clubs.

3. *Los Angeles Times*, 22 February 1996, A1.

4. I follow the standard practice of using the social titles "Mr." and "Ms." to refer to litigants.

5. Alan Lupo, "The Bully Who Would Be President," *Boston Globe,* 10 March 1996, 3.

6. Anne Ohman, "Buchanan's Words Speak Volumes," *Wisconsin State Journal,* 16 March 1996.

7. *President Bill Clinton's State of the Union Address,* House Chamber, The Capitol, 23 January 1996. Transcript by: Federal News Service, Available on Westlaw, 1996 WL 5793246. See also "Philadelphia Approves Public School Dress Code; Aiming to Instill Respect in Students, Nation's 5th-Largest District Will Let Schools Choose Uniforms," *Washington Post,* 9 May 2000, A05.

8. William Bennett, ed., *The Moral Compass: Stories for a Life's Journey* (New York: Simon & Schuster, 1995).

9. Allan Bloom, *The Closing of the American Mind* (New York: Touchstone Books, 1988).

10. Although there are some significant differences between the communitarianisms of Glendon and Sandel, they are both in agreement that our present problems can be traced, in part, to an unabashed privileging of individual rights. They focus, however, on different manifestations of the problem. Glendon regrets the spread of rights language to every conceivable social issue with the result, on her view, that individuals stand increasingly less willing to compromise and negotiate in a civil fashion.

Sandel, on the other hand, observes that respect for rights has come to mean that the state must remain neutral on any conception of the good life, thus prohibiting the larger community from making decisions aimed at promoting substantive goods.

11. Mary Ann Glendon, *Rights Talk: The Impoverishment of Political Discourse* (New York: Free Press, 1991), 107.

12. Michael J. Sandel, *Democracy's Discontent: America in Search of a Public Philosophy* (Cambridge, Mass.: Harvard University Press, 1996), 24–28. The irony, according to Sandel and Glendon, is that individuals are free not because they can choose their conception of the good life, but because they participate in such a conception. Hence, government neutrality and the demise of a shared tradition of goods functions not to give individuals more space for autonomy, but rather to eliminate the very condition of space for individual autonomy, namely community.

13. Glendon, *Rights Talk,* 14.

14. Ibid., 30.

15. Of course, it is worth noting that not all "public interests" are the same. One might want to distinguish public interests from corporate interests

—for example, community relocation to facilitate building a highway versus the development of a new Cadillac plant.

16. U.S. Constitution, amend. 1.

17. See, for example, Black's concurrence in *New York Times v. Sullivan*, 376 U.S. 254, 293 (1964) (emphasis added): "I base my vote to reverse on the belief that the First and Fourteenth Amendments not merely 'delimit' a State's power to award damages to 'public officials against critics of their official conduct' but completely prohibit a State from exercising such a power. The Court goes on to hold that a State can subject such critics to damages if 'actual malice' can be proved against them. 'Malice,' even as defined by the Court, is an elusive, abstract concept, hard to prove and hard to disprove. The requirement that malice be proved provides at best an evanescent protection for the right critically to discuss public affairs and certainly does not measure up to the sturdy safeguard embodied in the First Amendment. Unlike the Court, therefore, I vote to reverse exclusively on the ground that the Times and the individual defendants had an *absolute, unconditional constitutional right* to publish in the Times advertisement their criticisms of the Montgomery agencies and officials." For an interesting view on Black's absolutism, suggesting that it stems less from a commitment to absolutes *per se* and more from Black's unique understanding of his role as a Supreme Court justice, see Guido Calabresi, *A Common Law for the Age of Statutes* (Cambridge, Mass.: Harvard University Press, 1982), 180–81.

18. *Whitney v. California*, 274 U.S. 357, 375 (1927).

19. Perhaps, then, it is the "imminence" requirement that will do the majority of the work in protecting minority viewpoints. Considered from the mainstream, advocacy of communism may lead to serious evil, yet such advocacy is unlikely to take hold. So individuals may have as much and as radical free speech as they like—so long as the speech remains ineffective.

20. Indeed, Glendon takes issue with Brandeis: "What Justice Brandeis left out (and what American political actors generally ignore), however, is that supporters of a system that relies so heavily on public deliberation cannot afford to neglect the effective conditions for deliberation. The greatest obstacle to political renewal under present circumstances may not be an 'inert people' so much as the failure of persons in positions of leadership to provide models by personal example and to work actively to create opportunities for discussion." Glendon, *Rights Talk*, 179.

21. *Whitney*, 375 (emphasis added).

22. See, for example, Bruce Ackerman, *Social Justice in the Liberal State* (New Haven, Conn.: Yale University Press, 1980), 10–12, 43–45. Ackerman outlines an account of liberalism that requires the state to remain neutral between competing conceptions of the good life.

23. Sandel, *Democracy's Discontent,* 28.

24. Ibid., 90.

25. It is interesting to note that when Dewey discusses Brandeis in *Liberalism and Social Action,* he remembers Brandeis' opinion as a dissent, not a concurrence: "This [Brandeis' *Whitney* dissent] is the creed of a fighting liberalism. But the issue I am raising is connected with the fact that these words are found in a *dissenting,* a minority opinion of the Supreme Court of the United States. The public function of free individual thought and speech is clearly recognized in the words quoted. But the reception of the truth of the words is met by an obstacle: the old habit of defending liberty of thought and expression as something inhering in individuals apart from and even in opposition to social claims" (emphasis added). John Dewey, *The Later Works,* ed. Jo Ann Boydston, vol. 11, *1935–37, Essays, Liberalism and Social Action* 48 (Carbondale: Southern Illinois University Press, 1987).

26. See, e.g., Alexander Meiklejohn, *Free Speech and Its Relation to Self-Government* (New York: Harper Press, 1948).

27. Robert Post, *Constitutional Domains: Democracy, Community, Management* (Cambridge, Mass.: Harvard University Press, 1995), 275.

28. *Tinker v. Des Moines Independent Community School District,* 393 U.S. 503, 509 (1969).

29. For a critical look at the Supreme Court's use of deference with respect to claims of individual rights, see Daniel Solove, "The Darkest Domain: Deference, Judicial Review, and the Bill of Rights," 941 Iowa L. Rev. (1999), 84.

30. The language of Justice Black's concurring opinion in *Epperson v. Arkansas* is consonant with this claim. In the context of a decision in which the Supreme Court struck down an Arkansas statute prohibiting the teaching of evolution, Justice Black cautioned that he was "not ready to hold that a person hired to teach school children takes with him into the classroom a constitutional right to teach sociological, economic, political, or religious subjects that the school's managers do not want discussed." 393 U.S. 97, 113 (1968).

31. *Fraser v. Bethel School District,* 478 U.S. 675, 687 (1986).

32. Ibid., 680.

33. *Tinker.* In *Tinker,* three students were suspended from school for wearing black armbands in protest of U.S. involvement in the Vietnam War. While finding in favor of the students, the Supreme Court held that students and teachers maintained their First Amendment rights in the schoolhouse setting, although application of those rights required consideration of the special characteristics of the school environment. To prohibit expression covered under the First Amendment, it would be necessary for the school administration to show substantial interference with school discipline or the rights

of others. In *Fraser*, the administration claimed that Mr. Fraser's speech was indeed such a substantial interference.

34. *Fraser*, 683 (emphasis added).

35. Ibid.

36. For example, California adopted a policy that would allow schools not only to prohibit particular items of clothing, but also to mandate the wearing of a uniform (California Educational Code, Section 35294 [West 1993]). For a discussion of the constitutionality of such a code, see Alison Barbarosh, "Undressing The First Amendment in Public Schools," 28 Loyola L.A. L. Rev. (Summer 1995), 1415.

37. *Olesen v. Board of Education of School District No. 228*, 676 F. Supp. 820, 820 (1987).

38. Ibid., 823.

39. Ibid., 826.

40. Ibid.

41. Ibid., 826. (Quoting *Spence v. Washington*, footnote omitted.)

42. Ibid., 829.

43. Dewey, *The Later Works of John Dewey*, vol. 8, *1933, Essays, How We Think* (revised ed.), 147.

44. This is the suggestion of Principal Stephen Budihas, who believes that "schools have an obligation to keep pace with society's demands." Stephen J. Budihas, as quoted in *The Downsizing of America* (New York: Times Books, 1996), 245.

45. Ibid., 6.

46. "At present the universities are as uncongenial to teaching as the Mojave Desert to a clutch of Druid priests. If you want to restore a Druid priesthood, you cannot do it by offering prizes for Druid-of-the-year. If you want Druids, you must grow forests. There is no other way of setting about it." William Arrowsmith, as cited in Jay Rosenberg, *The Practice of Philosophy: A Handbook for Beginners* (Englewood Cliffs, N.J.: Prentice Hall, 1984), viii.

47. The Declaration of Independence, para 2.

48. I would argue that this reading is too narrow. The Declaration sets out the goals of government and the source of its legitimate authority. It sets out constitutional conditions.

49. Justice Stevens provides an interesting account of how the Court has incorporated aspects of the Declaration's theory of liberty through their interpretation of the Fifth Amendment's liberty clause. Justice John Paul Stevens, "A Century of Progress," in *The Bill of Rights in the Modern State,* ed. Geoffrey Stone and Richard Epstein (Chicago: University of Chicago Press, 1992), 23–24.

50. This is not to say that an unbridgeable categorical divide separates

questions of justice from questions of goodness. I leave open the question of their possible reconciliation.

51. See, for example, Richard Epstein, "Property, Speech, and the Politics of Distrust," in Stone and Epstein, eds, *The Bill of Rights*, 47–55.

52. Cf. U.S. Constitution, amend. 9 and 10.

53. Such arguments assume that government exists to provide protection against the perils of a state of nature, but respect for individual freedom requires it to do nothing beyond that. But the pressing question is one of content, what "individual freedom" can mean given prevailing social conditions.

54. Ralph Waldo Emerson, *Selections from Ralph Waldo Emerson: An Organic Anthology*, ed. Stephen Whicher (Boston: Houghton Mifflin Co., 1957), 349.

55. Emerson tended to prioritize the demands of nature over the demands of culture. As a consequence, his efforts focus on transforming the individual's relation to nature as opposed to the individual's relation with his society. As will become clear, I think he was naive in this respect.

56. It is this double movement of self-creation that Brandeis may have had in mind when he insisted in the *Whitney* concurrence that democracy is both a means and an end.

57. Dewey, *The Later Works of John Dewey*, vol. 5, *1929–1930, Essays, The Sources of a Science Education, Individualism, Old and New, and Construction and Criticism*, 80–81.

58. We will consider this problem again in the unlikely context of the so-called "counter-majoritarian difficulty." See chapter 5.

59. *The Downsizing of America*, 7.

60. Glendon, *Rights Talk*, 171.

61. Post, *Constitutional Domains*, 5.

62. Glendon, *Rights Talk*, 173.

63. Emerson, *Selections from Ralph Waldo Emerson*, 21.

64. John Dewey, *The Middle Works of John Dewey*, ed. Jo Ann Boydston, vol. 2, *1902–1903, Essays, The Child and the Curriculum, Studies in Logical Theory*, 26–27 (Carbondale: Southern Illinois University Press, 1976).

65. This thesis is advanced by Richard Schlatter in *Private Property: The History of an Idea* (New York: Russell and Russell, 1973), 151–161.

66. I am grateful to the editor of the *Transactions of the Charles S. Peirce Society* for permission to reproduce here and in the next chapter material in revised form from my article previously published therein: Michael Sullivan, "Pragmatism and Precedent: A Response to Dworkin," *Transactions of the Charles S. Peirce Society*, vol. 26(2), 1990.

67. Ronald Dworkin, *Law's Empire* (Cambridge, Mass.: Harvard University Press, Belknap Press, 1986), 160.

68. Immanuel Kant, *Grounding for the Metaphysics of Morals*, trans. James Ellington (Indianapolis.: Hackett Publishing Co., 1985), 36.

69. William James, *Pragmatism, The Works of William James* (Cambridge, Mass.: Harvard University Press, 1975), 97.

70. Dewey, *The Later Works of John Dewey*, vol. 5, *1929–1930, Essays, The Sources of a Science Education, Individualism, Old and New, and Construction and Criticism*, 57.

71. Dewey, *The Later Works of John Dewey*, vol. 13, *1938–1939, Essays, Experience and Education, Freedom and Culture, and Theory of Valuation*, 80–81.

72. Ibid., 174.

73. Dewey, *The Middle Works of John Dewey*, vol. 12, *1920, Essays, Reconstruction in Philosophy*, 186.

74. Dewey, *Freedom and Culture*, 87.

75. For a more fully developed account of this point in the context of allocating medical resources in democracy, see Michael Sullivan and John Lysaker, "Untying the Gag: The Claim of Reason in the World of Health Care Reform," in *Pragmatist Bioethics*, ed. Glenn McGee (Nashville, Tenn.: Vanderbilt University Press, 1999).

76. Dewey, *The Later Works of John Dewey*, vol. 2, *1925–1927, Essays, The Public and Its Problems*, 336.

77. Dewey, *The Later Works of John Dewey*, vol. 14, *1939–1941, Essays*, 122.

78. Dworkin, *Law's Empire*, 160 (emphasis added).

79. Dewey, *The Middle Works of John Dewey*, vol. 10, *1916–1917, Essays*, 45.

2. TAKING RIGHTS AND PRAGMATISM SERIOUSLY

1. Dworkin, *Law's Empire*, 153. A semantic theory, according to Dworkin, presupposes that "we can argue sensibly with one another if, but only if, we all accept and follow the same criteria for deciding when our claims are sound," *Law's Empire*, 45. Realism is a semantic theory to the extent it suggests that there is, albeit largely unrecognized, such a shared criterion in legal argumentation, namely that disagreements about the truth or falsity of legal propositions are simply differing predictions as to what the court will decide in future cases. Pragmatism, on the contrary, is an interpretive rather than semantic theory inasmuch as it recognizes we can and do have legitimate disagreements over questions of law despite employing different criteria in the very development of our understanding of what the law is. *Law's Empire*, 46.

2. Ibid., 94.

3. In using the term "pragmatism," I do not mean to imply that Dewey is

speaking for all pragmatists, although I expect many other pragmatists would be equally hostile to Dworkin's formulation of pragmatism. Dewey's philosophy, for instance, would be in agreement with Roscoe Pound's pragmatic philosophy in saying that judges should not apply law without concern for past decisions (as, according to Dworkin, pragmatic judges desire to do), although they should try to be aware of the "special circumstances" which make each case unique. See Roscoe Pound, *An Introduction to the Philosophy of Law* (New Haven, Conn.: Yale University Press, 1954), 69–71. For a detailed account of the relation between the pragmatism of Dewey and Pound, see Terry di Filippo, "Pragmatism, Interest Theory and Legal Philosophy: The Relation of James and Dewey to Roscoe Pound," *Transactions of the Charles S. Peirce Society,* vol. 24 (1988), 487–508.

4. Dworkin, *Law's Empire,* 151 (emphasis added). Dworkin has continued to comment on pragmatism since the publication of his argument in *Law's Empire,* but he has not in any substantive way further developed that argument. Moreover, he continues to avoid facing up to the significant challenge posed to his caricature of pragmatism by classical American pragmatists, in particular Dewey. In neither his 1997 Order of the Coif Lecture published in the *Arizona State Law Journal* (29 Ariz. St. L.J. 431) nor in his paper presented in the 1997 symposium on fidelity in constitutional theory (65 Fordham L. Rev 1249) has Dworkin been willing to consider the efficacy of his claims against a more substantial version of pragmatism, although in the later piece he is at least careful to point out that we should not construe his attacks on legal pragmatism as attacks on what he calls philosophical pragmatism (presumably classical American pragmatism). The effect of the dissociation, however, is to render the former position weak and easily assailable while ignoring the substantial challenge posed by the latter.

In Dworkin's 2002 *Harvard Law Review* (115 Harv. L. Rev. 1655) discussion of Jules Coleman's *Practice of Principle* (Oxford, 2001). Dworkin lambastes Coleman for using the term pragmatist in a manner which has virtually no connection to the American pragmatist tradition. Although Dworkin is right in his critique of Coleman, there is no small irony in the fact that Dworkin himself routinely uses this strategy of dissociating his account of pragmatism from the spirit of genuine American pragmatism when he finds it convenient to do so. If Dworkin is to make good on his claims in *Law's Empire* to have shown the superiority of his model of law as integrity over both positivism and pragmatism, then he should respond to the most well-developed version of pragmatism available.

5. The frequent occurrence of this misquotation of Emerson has earned it a place in a well-known book of misquotations. See Paul F. Boller, Jr., and John George, *They Never Said It* (New York: Oxford University Press, 1989), 25.

6. Emerson, *Selections from Ralph Waldo Emerson*, 152 (emphasis added).

7. Dewey, *1929–1930, Essays, The Sources of a Science Education, Individualism, Old and New, and Construction and Criticism*, 109.

8. Dewey, *The Later Works of John Dewey*, vol. 1, *1925, Experience and Nature*, 57–58.

9. Dewey, *1925–1927, Essays, The Public and Its Problems*, 342.

10. Dewey, *1938–1939, Essays, Experience and Education, Freedom and Culture, and Theory of Valuation*, 79.

11. Dewey, *1929–1930, Essays, The Sources of a Science Education, Individualism, Old and New, and Construction and Criticism*, 56–57.

12. Dworkin, *Law's Empire*, 151.

13. Dewey, *1929–1930, Essays, The Sources of a Science Education, Individualism, Old and New, and Construction and Criticism*, 122.

14. Dewey, *1925–1927, Essays, The Public and Its Problems*, 336.

15. Dworkin, *Law's Empire*, 161.

16. Ibid., 162.

17. Ibid., 161 (emphasis added).

18. Dewey, *1925–1927, Essays, The Public and Its Problems*, 336.

19. Dewey, *1938–1939, Essays, Experience and Education, Freedom and Culture, and Theory of Valuation*, 244–45.

20. Dworkin, *Law's Empire*, 159–60.

21. Ibid., 158.

22. Ibid., 158–59.

23. Ibid., 159.

24. Ibid.

25. There is one qualification of this statement: The pragmatist may not apply precedent to cases she believes are similar if she believes that the previous decision failed as an effective remedy for the problems addressed in that case.

26. Dewey, *1938–1939, Essays, Experience and Education, Freedom and Culture, and Theory of Valuation*, 245.

27. Dewey, *1939–1941, Essays*, 116–17.

28. Dworkin, *Law's Empire*, 239.

29. Ibid., 399.

30. Ibid., 387.

31. Ibid., 399.

32. *Stare decisis* is a Latin term that refers to the Court's policy of adhering to precedent and avoiding unsettling established points of law. It is the "doctrine that, when court has once laid down a principle of law as applicable to a certain state of facts, it will adhere to that principle and apply it to all future cases, where facts are substantially the same; regardless of whether the parties

and property is the same." Black's Law Dictionary 1261 (5th ed. 1979). The requirement of *stare decisis* is to treat like cases alike, but of course this is precisely the issue before the judge: Is this a like case? To claim that pragmatic judges don't respect precedent, Dworkin would need to show that the cases where the judge abandoned precedent were sufficiently alike.

33. There are subtler inquiries here as well, such as whether the judiciary is the appropriate institution to remedy the issue presented.

34. Benjamin Cardozo, *The Nature of the Judicial Process* (New Haven, Conn.: Yale University Press, 1921), 150. In *The Nature of the Judicial Process,* Cardozo refers to the influence of James' lectures on pragmatism (12–13), and, as Posner has also noted in his monograph study on Cardozo, one can also sense the presence of Dewey lurking between the lines: "We are thinking of the end which the law serves, and fitting its rules to the task of service. This conception of the end of law as determining the direction of its growth, which was Jhering's great contribution to the theory of jurisprudence, finds its organon, its instrument, in the method of sociology. Not the origin, but the goal, is the main thing. There can be no wisdom in the choice of a path unless we know where it will lead. The teleological conception of his function must be ever in the judge's mind. This means, of course, that the juristic philosophy of the common law is at bottom the philosophy of pragmatism." Richard Posner, *Cardozo: A Study in Reputation* (Chicago: University of Chicago Press, 1993), 27.

35. Dewey, *1925, Experience and Nature*, 32.

36. Cardozo, *The Nature of the Judicial Process*, 165–67.

3. POSNER'S UNPRAGMATIC PRAGMATISM

1. The work published in this chapter is derived and modified from portions of a review article written with Daniel Solove and previously published in the *Yale Law Journal*. The portions used here come from Part I and Part II.C of that review for which I was the primary author, although we both contributed substantially to all parts of the project. See Michael Sullivan and Daniel J. Solove, "Can Pragmatism Be Radical? Richard Posner and Legal Pragmatism," 113 Yale L.J. 687.

2. Richard Posner, *Law, Pragmatism and Democracy* (Cambridge, Mass.: Harvard University Press, 2003).

3. Ibid., 2.

4. Ibid., 3.

5. Ibid., 4.

6. Ibid., 41.

7. Ibid., 4.

8. Ibid., 11.

9. Ibid., 13. Interestingly, Posner refers to Dewey as "Professor Dewey" when he wants to criticize Dewey's more radical ideas about democracy and politics.

10. Ibid.

11. Ibid., 50.

12. Ibid., 12.

13. Ibid., 3.

14. Ibid., 60.

15. Ibid., 77. Additionally, as Daniel Farber notes: "In the legal context, pragmatism implies a certain degree of eclecticism. Pragmatism provides no reason to exclude consideration of original intent, precedent, philosophy, social science, or anything else that might be appropriate and helpful in resolving a hard case." Daniel A. Farber, "Reinventing Brandeis: Legal Pragmatism for the Twenty-First Century," U. Ill. L. Rev. (1995), 163, 169.

16. Posner, *Law, Pragmatism and Democracy,* 77.

17. Ibid., 50.

18. Ibid., 11.

19. Ibid., 79–80.

20. Ibid.

21. Ibid.

22. Ibid., 55–56.

23. Richard Posner, *The Problematics of Moral and Legal Theory* (Cambridge, Mass.: Harvard University Press, 1999).

24. Richard Posner, *Public Intellectuals: A Study in Decline* (Cambridge, Mass.: Harvard University Press, 2002).

25. Dewey, *1925, Experience and Nature,* 17.

26. Dewey, *The Later Works of John Dewey,* vol. 4, *1929, The Quest for Certainty,* 11–12.

27. Dewey, *1925, Experience and Nature,* 34. "Empirical method finds and points to the operation of choice as it does to any other event. Thus it protects us from conversion of eventual functions into antecedent existence: a conversion that may be said to be the philosophic fallacy, whether it be performed in behalf of mathematical subsistences, esthetic essences, the purely physical order of nature, or God."

28. Dewey, *1920, Essays, Reconstruction in Philosophy,* 94.

29. Dewey, *The Middle Works of John Dewey,* vol. 3, *The Need for Recovery of Philosophy,* 46.

30. Dewey, *1925, Experience and Nature,* 18.

31. Dewey, *The Later Works of John Dewey,* vol. 14, *My Philosophy of Law,* 115, 117.

32. Dewey, *The Middle Works of John Dewey*, vol. 3, *Education Direct and Indirect*, 240, 240–41.

33. Pragmatists like John Lachs have taken a different approach in part due to a different understanding of the reasons for academic insularity. Lachs believes that the insularity is less a function of the subject matter that academics discuss and more a function of institutional structures that reward and punish their behavior. Instead of concluding, as Posner does, that academic discussions are insular and therefore unimportant, he concludes that they are important but insulated. Accordingly, his recommendation is not to have the public ignore the academy, but rather to have the academy stop ignoring the public. John Lachs, *A Community of Individuals*, 8–9 (New York: Routledge, 2002) ("If encouraging intellectuals to engage in public debate does not work, we may have to make it mandatory. As part of the job description of thinkers, writers, and scientists, such participation would become a matter of habit. To get things going, we might have to impose the obligation that each intellectual undertake two or three critical sallies a year. Mechanical as this sounds, it would tend to break the cycle of fear and withdrawal in which many of the most intelligent humans are now caught. In the long run, intellectuals have to understand that they are on the payroll of the community in order, among other things, to warn us about our ways, to help us see our practices in perspective, to present arguments against what we are bent on doing, and, again and again, to present interesting alternatives. Their job is to shake up state and institutional orthodoxies, instead of working to preserve them.").

34. Steven D. Smith, "The Pursuit of Pragmatism," 100 Yale L.J. (1990), 409.

35. See John J. Stuhr, "Democracy as a Way of Life," in *Philosophy and the Reconstruction of Culture: Pragmatic Essays after Dewey*, ed. John J. Stuhr (New York: SUNY Press, 1993), 37, 40 (internal citations omitted) (for Dewey, "philosophy is inherently criticism and reconstruction").

36. David Luban, *Legal Modernism* (Ann Arbor: University of Michigan Press, 1997), 138.

37. Thomas C. Grey, "What Good Is Legal Pragmatism?" in Brint and Weaver, eds. *Pragmatism in Law and Society*, 9, 12.

38. Charles Peirce, *The Essential Peirce, Selected Philosophical Writings: Vol. 1, 1867–1893*, ed. Nathan Houser and Christian Kloesel (Bloomington: Indiana University Press, 1992), 132.

39. William James, *Pragmatism and The Meaning of Truth* (Cambridge, Mass.: Harvard University Press, 1978). See also Ellen Suckiel, *The Pragmatic Philosophy of William James* (London: University of Notre Dame Press, 1984), 38–41.

40. Dewey gives a brief account of the development of pragmatism in an entry written for a cyclopedia of education. Dewey, *The Middle Works of John Dewey*, vol. 7, *Contributions to a Cyclopedia of Education*, 209, 326–29.

41. Dewey, *The Later Works of John Dewey*, vol. 17, *Preface to The Influence of Darwin on Philosophy*, 39, 40.

42. Ibid.

43. James, *Pragmatism and The Meaning of Truth*, 32.

44. Posner, *Law, Pragmatism and Democracy*, 79.

45. For movies, see Spike Lee, *Do The Right Thing;* Woody Allen, *Crimes and Misdemeanors*. In literature, examples include the works of George Orwell, Toni Morrison, Margaret Atwood, and Charles Dickens (whose works were quite popular in his day).

46. Posner, *Law, Pragmatism and Democracy*, 55–56.

47. Ibid., 3–4. Despite this observation, Posner continues to produce work in the "theoretical uplands" that makes the call for more work in the lowlands.

48. Ian Ayers, *Pervasive Prejudice? Unconventional Evidence of Race and Gender Discrimination* (Chicago: University of Chicago Press, 2001), 315–87 (discussing empirical effects of affirmative action at FCC auctions).

49. Posner, *Law, Pragmatism and Democracy*, 59 ("The ultimate criterion of pragmatic adjudication is reasonableness.").

50. "[M]any moral theories, some of them of considerable prestige in philosophy, have interpreted moral subject-matter in terms of norms, standards, ideals, which according to the authors of these theories, have no possible factual standing. 'Reasons' for adopting and following them then involve a 'reason' and 'rational' in a sense which is expressly asserted to be transcendent, *a priori*, supernal, 'other-worldly.'" Dewey, *The Later Works of John Dewey*, vol. 15, *Ethical Subject-Matter and Language*, 139.

51. The person credited for inception of American pragmatism, Charles S. Peirce, has pointed out that pragmatism as a theory of meaning insists that to understand a concept is to understand the conceivable sensible effects of that concept. This does not mean one cannot use words such as "justice," "fairness," and "equality," but that one must understand the meaning of the terms not by reference to Platonic forms, but by reference to the practical consequences they entail. Peirce, *The Essential Peirce*, 132. See also Brian Leiter, "Rethinking Legal Realism: Toward a Naturalized Jurisprudence," 76 Tex. L. Rev. (1997), 267, 305 ("[P]ragmatism clearly has nothing against distinctions, definitions, coherence, abstract argument, or theoretical edifices: it is at least an open question whether or not these tools of the intellect are or are not useful for human purposes.").

52. Dewey, *The Later Works of John Dewey*, vol. 12, *1938, Logic: The*

Theory of Inquiry, 1, 216–17. As Margaret Radin correctly argues: "[I]deal theory is also necessary, because we need to know what we are trying to achieve. In other words, our visions and nonideal decisions, our theory and practice, paradoxically constitute each other." Margaret Jane Radin, "The Pragmatist and the Feminist," 63 S. Cal. L. Rev. (1990), 1699, in Brint and Weaver, eds., *Pragmatism in Law and Society,* 127, 129.

53. See, e.g., Daniel A. Farber, "Shocking the Conscience: Pragmatism, Moral Reasoning, and the Judiciary," 16 Const. Comment. (1999), 675, 689 (noting that "moral conceptualism is an intellectual tumor that Posner would like to remove. But as with certain tumors, it is doubtful that we can excise every trace of these moral conceptions from the legal mind without fatally impairing vital functions.").

54. Dewey, *The Middle Works of John Dewey,* vol. 14, *Human Nature and Conduct,* 48.

55. Ibid.

56. Ibid.

57. Ibid.

58. Ibid., 43.

59. Ibid.

60. Ibid., 47.

61. Ibid., 90.

62. Ibid., 17–18.

63. Dewey, John. *The Early Works, 1882–1898,* ed. Jo Ann Boydston, vol. 5, *Evolution and Ethics,* 34, 48 (Carbondale: Southern Illinois University Press, 1969–72).

64. Ibid.

65. Dewey, *1925, Experience and Nature,* 312.

66. Ibid.

67. Dworkin, *Law's Empire,* 161.

68. David Luban, "What's Pragmatic About Legal Pragmatism?" 18 Cardozo L. Rev. (1996), 43.

69. Posner, *Law, Pragmatism and Democracy,* 71.

70. Ibid., 59–60.

71. Of course, it is still no easy matter to determine whether a precedent applies along the formalist model. One has to determine that the present facts are similar in a relevant way to the facts of the past case; there can be, therefore, great difficulties in predicting the action of the courts even if they maintain a staunch commitment to taking precedent seriously.

72. Posner, *Law, Pragmatism and Democracy,* 60. Margaret Radin offers a critique of Dworkin along similar lines. See Radin, "The Pragmatist and the Feminist," in Brint and Weaver, eds., *Pragmatism in Law and Society,* 145–47.

73. Posner, *Law, Pragmatism and Democracy,* 60.

74. Ibid., 6.

75. Ibid., 71.

76. Ibid.

77. Ibid., 120.

78. Ibid., 105.

79. Ibid., 55.

80. Brian Z. Tamanaha, "Pragmatism in U.S. Legal Theory: Its Application to Normative Jurisprudence, Sociolegal Studies, and the Fact-Value Distinction," 41 Am. J. Juris. (1996), 315, 328.

81. Ibid.

82. Lynn A. Baker, " 'Just Do It': Pragmatism and Progressive Social Change," 78 Va. L. Rev. (1992), 697, in Brint and Weaver, eds., *Pragmatism in Law and Society,* 99, 115.

83. See Daniel A. Farber, "Legal Pragmatism and the Constitution," 72 Minn. L. Rev. (1988), 1331, 1350 ("For the pragmatist the analysis must start—but not finish—with an examination of our constitutional text, history, and traditions.").

84. Holmes wrote: "The law embodies the story of a nation's development through many centuries, and it cannot be dealt with as if it contained only the axioms and corollaries of a book of mathematics. In order to know what it is, we must know what it has been, and what it tends to become." Oliver Wendell Holmes, *The Common Law 1* (Boston: Little, Brown & Co., 1886).

85. Dewey, *Essays, The Public and Its Problems,* 235, 336.

86. Ibid.

87. Ibid., 217.

88. Dewey, *1929, The Quest for Certainty,* 217.

89. Dewey, *1925, Experience and Nature,* 299.

90. Dewey, *The Middle Works of John Dewey,* vol. 2, *The Evolutionary Method as Applied to Morality,* 3, 26–27.

91. Ibid.

92. Posner, *Law, Pragmatism and Democracy,* 11.

93. Ibid., 76, 79.

94. Ibid., 121.

95. Richard Posner, *Overcoming Law* (Cambridge, Mass.: Harvard University Press, 1995), 192.

96. Posner, *Law, Pragmatism and Democracy,* 121.

97. Ibid., 122.

98. Ibid., 123.

99. Ibid., 86.

100. Ibid., 92.

101. Ibid., 91.

102. Ibid., 92.

103. U.S. 483 (1954).

104. Posner, *Law, Pragmatism and Democracy,* 198.

105. See, e.g., Jeffrey Rosen, Book Review, "Overcoming Posner," 105 Yale L.J. (1995), 581, 596 ["The project of independent empirical inquiry is so inherently aggressive, and the likelihood that legislatures (especially state legislatures) have acted sloppily or irrationally is so great, that a pragmatist such as Posner might find it hard, in practice, to restrain himself from substituting his own judgment for that of the political branches by following the facts to their logical conclusion."].

106. Solove, "The Darkest Domain", 941, 1018.

107. Daniel A. Farber, "Legal Pragmatism and the Constitution," 72 Minn. L. Rev. (1988), 1331, 1347–48.

108. Posner, *Law, Pragmatism and Democracy,* 291–321.

109. Ibid., 296.

110. Ibid., 298.

111. Ibid.

112. Ibid.

113. Ibid.

114. Ibid., 296.

115. Ibid.

116. Ibid., 298.

117. Ibid., 298–99.

118. Ibid., 304.

119. See Curt Gentry, *J. Edgar Hoover: The Man and the Secrets* (New York: W. W. Norton & Company, 1991), 75–76, 83, 93.

120. See Charles H. McCormick, *Seeing Reds: Federal Surveillance of Radicals in the Pittsburgh Mill District, 1917–1921,* (Pittsburgh: University of Pittsburgh Press, 1997), 120.

121. See Frank J. Donner, *The Age of Surveillance: The Aims and Methods of America's Political Intelligence System* (New York: Knopf, distributed by Random House, 1980), 33.

122. Gentry, *J. Edgar Hoover: The Man and the Secrets,* 76.

123. See Richard Gid Powers, *Secrecy and Power: The Life of J. Edgar Hoover* (New York: Free Press, 1987), 79–80.

124. Eric K. Yamamoto et al., *Race, Rights, and Reparations: Law and the Japanese American Internment* (New York: Aspen Publishers, 2001), 38; see also Eugene V. Rostow, "The Japanese American Cases—A Disaster," 54 Yale L.J. (1945), 489.

125. U.S. 214 (1944).

126. Ibid., 216.

127. Posner, *Law, Pragmatism and Democracy,* 294.

128. See *Personal Justice Denied: Report of the Commission on Wartime Relocation and Internment of Civilians* (Washington, D.C.: U.S. Government Printing Office, 1982).

129. See, e.g., Sheryl Gay Stolberg, "Transcripts Detail Secret Questioning in 50's by McCarthy," *New York Times,* 6 May 2003.

130. See Ellen Schrecker, *The Age of McCarthyism: A Brief History with Documents* (Boston: Bedford Books of St. Martin's Press, 1994), 92–94; Seth I. Kreimer, "Sunlight, Secrets, and Scarlet Letters: The Tension Between Privacy and Disclosure in Constitutional Law," 140 U. Pa. L. Rev. (1991), 1, 13–71.

131. Schrecker, *The Age of McCarthyism,* 56, 76–84.

132. Ibid., 10.

133. Ibid., 92–94.

134. Richard A. Posner, *Not a Suicide Pact: The Constitution in a Time of National Emergency* (Oxford: Oxford University Press, 2006), 50.

135. Ibid.

136. Ibid., 51.

137. Posner, *Law, Pragmatism and Democracy,* 312–15.

138. Posner, *Not a Suicide Pact,* 51.

139. In his more recent work, Posner countenances such a possibility in passing, but does not go further. He notes: "The post–9/11 sweeps that I mentioned caught a number of innocent fish in their nets, perhaps avoidably, to the detriment of good relations between the intelligence services and the American Muslim community." *Not a Suicide Pact,* 50.

140. See, e.g., Eric Lichtblau, "U.S. Report Faults the Roundup of Illegal Immigrants After 9/11," *New York Times,* 3 June 2003.

141. Akhil Reed Amar, *The Constitution and Criminal Procedure* (New Haven, Conn.: Yale University Press, 1997), 31 ("The core of the Fourth Amendment . . . is neither a warrant nor probable cause but reasonableness.").

142. Posner, *Law, Pragmatism and Democracy.*

143. *Brinegar v. United States,* 338 U.S. 160, 175–76 (1949).

144. Posner, *Law, Pragmatism and Democracy,* 303.

145. Ibid., 69.

146. See Raymond S. R. Ku, "The Founder's Privacy: The Fourth Amendment and the Power of Technological Surveillance," 86 Minn. L. Rev. (2002), 1325.

147. Christopher Slobogin, "The World Without a Fourth Amendment," 39 UCLA L. Rev. (1991), 1, 17.

148. *McDonald v. United States,* 335 U.S. 451, 455–56 (1948).

149. Louis Fisher, "Congress and the Fourth Amendment," 21 Ga. L. Rev. (1986), 107, 115 ("The spirit and letter of the fourth amendment counseled against the belief that Congress intended to authorize a 'fishing expedition' into private papers on the possibility that they might disclose a crime.").

150. U.S. Constitution, amend. IV.

151. Tracey Maclin, "When the Cure for the Fourth Amendment is Worse than the Disease," 68 S. Cal. L. Rev. (1994), 1, 8–9; Leonard W. Levy, *Origins of the Bill of Rights* (New Haven, Conn.: Yale University Press, 1999), 158.

152. Silas J. Wasserstrom and Louis Michael Seidman, "The Fourth Amendment as Constitutional Theory," 77 Geo. L.J. (1988), 19, 82.

153. Levy, *Origins of the Bill of Rights*, 150; William J. Stuntz, "The Substantive Origins of Criminal Procedure," 105 Yale L.J. (1995), 393, 406.

154. Posner, *Law, Pragmatism and Democracy*, 98.

155. Dewey, *1925, Experience and Nature*, 43.

156. Ibid., 47–60.

157. Ibid., 60.

158. Ibid., 120.

159. John Dewey, *The Later Works of John Dewey*, vol. 5, *1929–30, Individualism Old and New*, 115–16.

160. Dewey, *1925, Experience and Nature*, 308.

161. John Dewey, *The Later Works of John Dewey*, vol. 11, *1935–37, Essays, Democracy and Educational Administration*, 217.

162. Hilary Putnam, "A Reconsideration of Dewey and Democracy," 63 S. Cal. L. Rev. (1990), 1671, 1671.

163. Dewey, *Democracy and Educational Administration*, 217.

164. Stuhr, "Democracy as a Way of Life," 42.

165. Ibid.

166. Ibid., 54.

167. Ibid., 45.

168. Ibid., 39.

169. Ibid., 40.

170. John Dewey, *The Later Works of John Dewey*, vol. 11, *1935–37, Essays, Democracy is Radical*, 298–299 (italics removed).

171. William R. Caspary, *Dewey on Democracy* (Ithaca, N.Y.: Cornell University Press, 2000), 8.

172. Dewey, *1925–1927, Essays, The Public and Its Problems*, 327.

173. Ibid., 364.

174. Dewey, *Democracy is Radical*, 298 (italics removed).

175. Posner, *Law, Pragmatism and Democracy*, 105–106.

176. Robert B. Westbrook, *John Dewey and American Democracy* (Ithaca, N.Y.: Cornell University Press, 1991), 187–88.

177. Dewey, *1925, Experience and Nature,* 29 ("When intellectual experience and its material are taken to be primary, the cord that binds experience and nature is cut.").

178. Ibid., 26.

179. Ibid.

180. Dewey, *1920, Essays, Reconstruction in Philosophy,* 145.

181. Stuhr, "Democracy as a Way of Life," 46.

182. Ibid., 47.

183. Ibid.

184. Dewey, *1935–37, Essays, Liberalism and Social Action,* 41.

185. Dewey, *Democracy and Educational Administration,* 217, 219.

186. Dewey, *Freedom and Culture,* 151–52.

187. James Campbell, *Understanding John Dewey* (Chicago: Open Court Press, 1995), 37–38. Posner repeatedly discusses the influence of Darwin on pragmatism. See Posner, *Law, Pragmatism and Democracy,* 4–5, 9–10, 31–32.

188. Dewey, *Democracy Is Radical,* 298–99 (italics removed).

4. TOWARD A RECONSTRUCTIVE PRAGMATISM

1. Anthony Kronman, "Precedent and Tradition," 99 Yale L.J. (1990), 1033.

2. Dewey, *1925, Experience and Nature,* 18.

3. Dewey, *The Later Works of John Dewey,* vol. 16, *1949–1952, Essays, Modern Philosophy,* 415.

4. Ibid.

5. James, *Pragmatism, The Works of William James,* 97.

6. Dworkin makes a related argument. He claims that classical English jurisprudence made a distinction between "ethical jurisprudence," dedicated to studying what the law should be, and "analytic" jurisprudence, dedicated to determining the meaning of key legal terms. English jurisprudence focused on "analytic" questions and failed to acknowledge law's dependence on moral philosophy. According to Dworkin, the questions of justification we find most vexing cannot be satisfactorily addressed by explicating legal concepts alone; they require investigation of moral concepts. Ronald Dworkin, *Taking Rights Seriously* (Cambridge, Mass.: Harvard University Press, 1977), 2–3.

7. I am indebted to a lecture by Alasdair MacIntyre for this example.

8. David Lewis, *Philosophical Papers* (London: Oxford University Press, 1983), x. A. Mitchell Polinsky offers a similar assessment of the contribution of economic approaches to law: "However, as we have seen in specific applications, the inability of the legal system to achieve every objective does not mean that the economic approach to law is necessarily indeterminate and unhelpful. On the contrary, the fact that there are many goals that the legal system might

be viewed as trying to accomplish makes economic analysis all the more helpful in determining what the tradeoffs are among the goals and how to strike an appropriate balance." A. Mitchell Polinsky, *An Introduction to Law and Economics* (Boston: Little, Brown, 1983), 120–21.

9. Thomas Grey comes to this conclusion concerning the application of pragmatic philosophy: "But I must disclaim from the start any suggestion that pragmatist theory by itself can supply the pragmatist with any solution to the harassment problem. My pragmatism tells me that there is no uniquely correct solution nor is any particular solution dictated by pragmatist precepts or methods." Grey, "What Good Is Legal Pragmatism?" 91.

10. Richard Rorty, *Contingency, Irony, and Solidarity* (Cambridge: Cambridge University Press, 1989), 80.

11. Ibid., 94.

12. Dewey, *My Philosophy of Law*, 116–123 passim.

13. Dewey notes that law is one of the most conservative of human institutions. Dewey, "Does Human Nature Change," in *1938–1939, Essays, Experience and Education, Freedom and Culture, and Theory of Valuation*, 292. "The force of lag in human life is enormous. . . . Political and legal institutions may be altered, even abolished; but the bulk of popular thought which has been shaped to their pattern persists." *The Middle Works of John Dewey*, vol. 14, *1922, Human Nature and Conduct*, 77. Dewey also notes that that antiquated legal institutions and patterns of mind persist in the present. *The Later Works of John Dewey*, vol. 11, *1935–1937, Essays, Liberalism and Social Action*, 55. "[Marx] showed in considerable detail that the cause of the lag is subordination of productive forces to legal and political conditions holding over from a previous regime of production." *1938–1939, Essays, Experience and Education, Freedom and Culture, and Theory of Valuation*, 120. "Law is usually more backward than public opinion. Especially is this true of the decisions of the courts, because these are based in part upon custom which in turn reflects past opinion and past habits of thought." *The Later Works of John Dewey*, vol. 7, *1932, Ethics*, 396.

14. "This creed [laissez-faire liberalism] is still powerful in this country. The earlier doctrine of 'natural rights,' superior to legislative action, has been given a definitely economic meaning by the courts, and used by judges to destroy social legislation passed in the interest of a real, instead of purely formal, liberty of contract." Dewey, *1935–1937, Essays, Liberalism and Social Action*, 26.

15. For a detailed account of the incongruity between the fact of increasing social interdependence and continued adherence to antiquated ideals of individualism, see Dewey, *1929–1930, Essays, The Sources of a Science Education, Individualism, Old and New, and Construction and Criticism*, 90–99.

16. See Thomas Krattenmaker and L. Powe, Jr., "Symposium: Emerging Media Technology and the First Amendment: Converging First Amendment Principles for converging communications Media," 104 Yale L.J. (May 1995), 1729. See also "Note: The Message in the Medium: The First Amendment on the Information Superhighway," 107 Harv, L. Rev. (March 1994), 1062.

17. *Roth v. United States,* 354 U.S. 476, 489 (1957).

18. Dewey, *The Later Works of John Dewey,* vol. 10, *1934, Art as Experience,* 303.

19. I am grateful to the Pennsylvania State University Press for permission to reproduce material here in revised form from my article published in their journal: Michael Sullivan, "Law's Literature: Reconstruction or Diversion," *Journal of Speculative Philosophy* 12.4 (1998). Copyright 1998 by The Pennsylvania State University.

20. I am indebted to several conversations with Daniel Solove that helped me in thinking through the relationship between law and literature.

21. Patricia Williams, *The Alchemy of Race and Rights* (Cambridge, Mass.: Harvard University Press, 1991). For an excellent account of the storytelling movement which generally emphasizes the positive contributions of Williams and others, see Daniel Farber and Suzanna Sherry, "Telling Stories Out of School: An Essay on Legal Narratives," 45 Stan. L. Rev. (April 1993), 807.

22. See Richard Weissberg, *The Failure of the Word* (New Haven, Conn.: Yale University Press, 1984); James Boyd White, *Heracles' Bow: Essays on the Rhetoric and Poetics of the Law* (Madison: University of Wisconsin Press, 1985); and Rorty, *Contingency, Irony, and Solidarity.*

23. Rorty, *Contingency, Irony, and Solidarity,* 94.

24. Stanley Fish, "Fish v. Fiss," in Stanley Fish, *Doing What Comes Naturally: Change, Rhetoric, and the Practice of Theory in Literary and Legal Studies* (Durham, N.C.: Duke University Press, 1989), 129.

25. Stanley Fish, "Don't Know Much About the Middle Ages," in Fish, *Doing What Comes Naturally,* 303.

26. Ibid., 301.

27. Ibid., 304.

28. Stanley Fish, "Almost Pragmatism: The Jurisprudence of Richard Posner, Richard Rorty, and Ronald Dworkin," in Brint and Weaver, eds., *Pragmatism in Law and Society,* 79–80.

29. Ibid., 68.

30. Ibid., 60.

31. Rorty, *Contingency, Irony, and Solidarity,* 91.

32. Ibid., 69.

33. Rorty, "The Banality of Pragmatism and the Poetry of Justice," 93.

34. Rorty, *Contingency, Irony, and Solidarity,* 63.

35. One can see this tendency at work in Rorty's discussion of the role that scientific discourse can play in furthering liberalism. He concludes it can play only a minor role because such discourses are too difficult to master and thereby participate in. Accordingly, he recommends "switching attention to the areas which are at the forefront of culture, those which excite the imagination of the young, namely, art and utopian politics." Ibid., 52.

36. Dewey, *1925, Experience and Nature,* 410.

37. Ibid., 305.

38. Ibid., 410.

39. Ibid., 18–19.

40. Dewey, *1929, The Quest for Certainty,* 196.

41. John Dewey, *1918–1919, Essays,* 346. The discussion by Professors Edel and Flowers in the preface to vol. 7 of Dewey's later works was very helpful to me in considering this point. Dewey, *1932, Ethics,* 196.

42. In light of this commitment, shared by pragmatists generally, it is difficult to understand why Dworkin would charge pragmatists with a lack of concern for history in executing their jurisprudence.

43. Dewey's position is contrary to the position adopted by Stanley Fish in a review of Richard Posner's work in which he claims that practices, especially practices of theory or anti-theory, have no effect on law. It seems as though Fish guarantees the result he seeks theoretically by rendering legal practice discrete and autonomous in such a way that "it" can only effect itself. He then places all meaningful discussion of theory or philosophical critique on the "outside." See Fish, "Almost Pragmatism," 55, 61, 68, 79–80.

44. Grey, "What Good Is Legal Pragmatism?" 22–26.

5. RECONSTRUCTING JUDICIAL REVIEW

1. One of Dewey's great contributions to value theory is to recognize that values are both means and ends.

2. Curiously enough, Dewey's protégé Sidney Hook took up the question of judicial review in a chapter of his book on the paradoxes of freedom a year prior to Bickel's celebrated book. Hook's analysis, however, which concluded the Court was in fact unacceptably undemocratic, seems to have attracted little attention in legal circles. Sidney Hook, *The Paradoxes of Freedom* (Berkeley: University of California Press, 1962).

3. Alexander Bickel, *The Least Dangerous Branch: The Supreme Court at the Bar of Politics* (New Haven, Conn.: Yale University Press, 1986) 16–17 (emphasis mine). First published in 1962 by Bobbs-Merrill in Indianapolis.

4. "It is a premise we deduce not merely from the fact of a written

constitution but from the history of the race, and ultimately as a moral judgment of the good society, that government should serve not only what we conceive from time to time to be our immediate material needs but also certain enduring values." Ibid., 24.

5. "The heart of the democratic faith is government by the consent of the governed. The further premise is not incompatible that the good society not only will want to satisfy the immediate needs of the greatest number but also will strive to support and maintain enduring general values. I have followed the view that the elected institutions are ill fitted . . . to perform the latter task." Ibid., 27.

6. Given that Bickel understands it in terms of frustration of the present majority, or what he calls the "actual people."

7. For a well-developed argument along these lines, see Robert Paul Wolff, *In Defense of Anarchism* (New York: Harper & Row, 1970), 21–67.

8. Bickel, *The Least Dangerous Branch*, 24.

9. Ibid., fn 3.

10. Ibid., 66–69.

11. Ibid., 68.

12. Ibid.

13. Ibid., (emphasis added).

14. This interpretation of Bickel's priorities is consistent with his earlier statement: "Such a government must be principled as well as responsible, but it must be felt to be the one without having ceased to be the other, and unless it is responsible it cannot in fact be stable, and is not in my view morally supportable." Ibid., 29.

15. The other crucial question is, where do these principles come from? Are they transcendent, part of the evolving history of human beings, or particular to the history of our constitutional democracy? Bickel seems undecided on this issue as well, despite continual appeals to the historical evolution of such principles. More interesting still, his worry seems to be that the principles, which he says must take the form of absolutes, will be too pure for hasty application to a sullied society. An equally pressing critical worry is not that the principles are too pure, but that they are too sullied. If your access to the good is social and historical and that history has produced frightful absolutes, then the deep worry is that your regulative ideals will be equally contaminated. So the point of prudence, one may argue contra Bickel, is not opposition to principle because the phase-in process is difficult, but the attempt to cultivate critical understanding of a principle through attention to its historical development in changing circumstances.

16. Ibid., 239.

17. Ibid.

18. Bruce Ackerman, *We the People: Foundations* (Cambridge, Mass.: Harvard University Press, Belknap Press, 1991), 6.

19. Ibid., 57.

20. Publius was the signatory of the famous Federalist Papers published to garner support for the Constitution. Ackerman invokes the spirit of Publius in support of his account of dualist democracy.

21. Admittedly, this is framed as the forward-looking question—what do we want our constitution to be?—and not Ackerman's treasured backward-looking question. But, as I try to suggest in "Vision Without Telos," unpublished paper on file with author, there is no simple severing of the descriptive and prescriptive dimensions of such inquiries.

22. It does, but the angst it creates may be worse.

23. John Hart Ely, *Democracy and Distrust: A Theory of Judicial Review* (Cambridge, Mass.: Harvard University Press, 1980).

24. Consider, for example, the Court's invalidation of Jim Crow laws. David Fremon, *The Jim Crow Laws and Racism in American History* (Berkeley Heights, N.J.: Enslow Press, 2000).

25. Bickel, *The Least Dangerous Branch,* 239.

26. These principles, though absolute, are apparently historically derived.

27. Post, *Constitutional Domains,* passim.

6. PRAGMATISM, GENEALOGY, AND DEMOCRACY

1. Dewey, *1925–1927, Essays, The Public and Its Problems,* 364.

SELECTED BIBLIOGRAPHY

Ackerman, Bruce. *Social Justice in the Liberal Stage.* New Haven, Conn.: Yale University Press, 1980.

——. *We the People: Foundations.* Cambridge, Mass.: Harvard University Press, Belknap Press, 1991.

Amar, Akhil Reed. *The Constitution and Criminal Procedure.* New Haven, Conn.: Yale University Press, 1997.

Arthur, John. *Words that Bind: Judicial Review and the Grounds of Modern Constitutional Theory.* Boulder, Colo.: Westview, 1995.

Bennett, William, ed. *The Moral Compass: Stories for a Life's Journey.* New York: Simon & Schuster, 1995.

Bickel, Alexander M. *The Morality of Consent.* New Haven, Conn.: Yale University Press, 1975.

——. *The Least Dangerous Branch: The Supreme Court at the Bar of Politics.* 2nd ed. New Haven, Conn.: Yale University Press, 1986.

Bloom, Allan. *The Closing of the American Mind.* New York: Touchstone Books, 1988.

Boller, Paul F., Jr., and John George. *The Never Said It.* New York: Oxford University Press, 1989.

Brint, Michael, and William Weaver, eds. *Pragmatism in Law and Society.* Boulder, Colo.: Westview, 1991.

Calabresi, Guido. *A Common Law for the Age of Statutes.* Cambridge, Mass.: Harvard University Press, 1982.

Cardozo, Benjamin N. *The Nature of the Judicial Process.* New Haven, Conn.: Yale University Press, 1921.

Cavell, Stanley. *Conditions Handsome and Unhandsome: The Constitution of Emersonian Perfectionism.* La Salle: Open Court, 1990.

Chafee, Zechariah, Jr. *Free Speech in the United States.* Cambridge, Mass.: Harvard University Press, 1948.

Coval, S. C., and Joseph C. Smith. *Law and Its Presuppositions: Actions, Agents and Rules.* London: Routledge & Kegan Paul, 1986.

Curtis, Michael Kent. *No State Shall Abridge the Fourteenth Amendment and the Bill of Rights.* Durham, N.C.: Duke University Press, 1986.

Dewey, John. *The Early Works, 1882–1898.* Edited by Jo Ann Boydston. Carbondale: Southern Illinois University Press, 1969–72.

——. *The Middle Works, 1899–1924.* Edited by Jo Ann Boydston. Carbondale: Southern Illinois University Press, 1976–83.

——. *The Later Works, 1925–1953.* Edited by Jo Ann Boydston. Carbondale: Southern Illinois University Press, 1981–91.

Dworkin, Ronald. *Law's Empire.* Cambridge, Mass.: Harvard University Press, Belknap Press, 1986.

——. *Freedom's Law: The Moral Reading of the American Constitution.* Cambridge, Mass.: Harvard University Press, 1996.

——. *Taking Rights Seriously.* Cambridge, Mass.: Harvard University Press, 1997.

——. *Justice In Robes.* Cambridge, Mass.: Harvard University Press, 2006.

Ely, John Hart. *Democracy and Distrust: A Theory of Judicial Review.* Cambridge, Mass.: Harvard University Press, 1980.

Emerson, Ralph Waldo. *Selections from Ralph Waldo Emerson: an Organic Anthology.* Edited by Stephen E. Whicher. Boston: Houghton Mifflin Co., 1957.

Fish, Stanley. *Doing What Comes Naturally: Change, Rhetoric, and the Practice of Theory in Literary and Legal Studies.* Durham, N.C.: Duke University Press, 1989.

——. *There's No Such Thing as Free Speech and It's a Good Thing, Too.* Oxford: Oxford University Press, 1994.

——. *The Trouble with Principle.* Cambridge, Mass.: Harvard University Press, 1999.

Fremon, David. *The Jim Crow Laws and Racism in American History.* Berkeley Heights, N.J.: Enslow Press, 2000.

Fuller, Lon L. *The Morality of Law.* Revised edition. New Haven, Conn.: Yale University Press, 1969.

Glendon, Mary Ann. *Rights Talk: The Impoverishment of Political Discourse.* New York: The Free Press, 1991.

Golding, M. P., ed. *The Nature of Law: Readings in Legal Philosophy.* New York: Random House, 1966.

Goldstein, Laurence, ed. *Precedent in Law.* Oxford: Clarendon Press, 1987; reprint, 1991.

Gouinlock, James. *John Dewey's Philosophy of Value.* New York: Humanities Press, 1972.

——. *Excellence in Public Discourse: John Stuart Mill, John Dewey, and Social Intelligence.* New York: Teachers College Press, 1986.

Grey, Thomas C. *The Wallace Stevens Case: Law and the Practice of Poetry.* Cambridge, Mass.: Harvard University Press, 1991.

Hart, H. L. A. *The Concept of Law.* Oxford: Clarendon Press, 1961; reprint, 1995.

——. *Essays in Jurisprudence and Philosophy.* Oxford: Clarendon Press, 1983.

Holmes, Oliver Wendell, Jr. *Representative Opinions of Mr. Justice Holmes.* Arranged by Alfred Lief. New York: Vanguard Press, 1931.

——. *The Essential Holmes: Selections from the Letters, Speeches, Judicial Opinions, and Other Writings of Oliver Wendell Holmes, Jr.* Edited by Richard A. Posner. Chicago: The University of Chicago Press, 1992.

Hook, Sidney. *The Paradoxes of Freedom.* Berkeley: University of California Press, 1962.

——, ed. *Human Values and Economic Policy: A Symposium.* New York: New York University Press, 1967.

Irons, Peter. *The Courage of Their Convictions.* New York: Free Press, 1988.

James, William. *Pragmatism, The Works of William James.* Cambridge, Mass.: Harvard University Press, 1975.

Kalman, Laura. *The Strange Career of Legal Liberalism.* New Haven, Conn.: Yale University Press, 1996.

Kant, Immanuel. *Grounding for the Metaphysics of Morals.* Translated by James W. Ellington. 2nd ed. Indianapolis: Hackett Publishing Company, 1985.

Kaufman-Osborn, Timothy V. *Politics/Sense/Experience: A Pragmatic Inquiry into the Promise of Democracy.* Ithaca, N.Y.: Cornell University Press, 1991.

Kelman, Mark. *A Guide to Critical Legal Studies.* Cambridge, Mass.: Harvard University Press, 1987.

Kennedy, Duncan. *A Critique of Adjudication.* Cambridge, Mass.: Harvard University Press, 1997.

Kevelson, Roberta. *Peirce, Paradox, Praxis: The Image, the Conflict, and the Law.* New York: Mouton de Gruyter, 1990.

Lachs, John. *The Relevance of Philosophy to Life.* Nashville, Tenn.: Vanderbilt University Press, 1995.

Lewis, David. *Philosophical Papers: Volume I.* Oxford: Oxford University Press, 1983.

MacIntyre, Alasdair. *After Virtue: A Study in Moral Theory.* London: Gerald Duckworth & Co., 1981; Notre Dame, Ind.: University of Notre Dame Press, 1981.

——. *Whose Justice? Which Rationality?* Notre Dame, Ind.: University of Notre Dame Press, 1988.

——. *Three Rival Versions of Moral Enquiry: Encyclopaedia, Genealogy, and Tradition.* Notre Dame, Ind.: University of Notre Dame Press, 1990.

McGee, Glenn, ed. *Pragmatic Bioethics.* Nashville, Tenn.: Vanderbilt University Press, 1999.

Meiklejohn, Alexander. *Free Speech and its Relation to Self-Government.* New York: Harper Press, 1948.

Minow, Martha. *Making All the Difference: Inclusion, Exclusion, and American Law.* Ithaca, N.Y.: Cornell University Press, 1990.

Nagel, Robert F. *Constitutional Cultures: The Mentality and Consequences of Judicial Review.* Berkeley: University of California Press, 1989.

Peirce, Charles. *The Essential Peirce, Selected Philosophical Writings: Vol. 1 (1867–1893).* Edited by Nathan Houser and Christian Kloesel. Indianapolis: Indiana University Press, 1992.

——. *The Essential Peirce, Selected Philosophical Writings: Vol. 2 (1893–1913).* Edited by the Peirce Edition Project. Indianapolis: Indiana University Press, 1998.

Pennock, J. Roland, and John W. Chapman, eds. *Constitutionalism NOMOS XX.* New York: New York University Press, 1979.

——, ed. *Justification: NOMOS XXVIII.* New York: New York University Press, 1986.

——, ed. *Authority Revisited: NOMOS XXIX.* New York: New York University, 1987.

Perry, H. W., Jr. *Deciding to Decide: Agenda Setting in the United States Supreme Court.* Cambridge, Mass.: Harvard University Press, 1991.

Polinsky, A. Mitchell. *An Introduction to Law and Economics.* Boston: Little, Brown and Company, 1983.

Posner, Richard A. *Law and Literature: A Misunderstood Relation.* Cambridge, Mass.: Harvard University Press, 1988.

——. *Cardozo: A Study in Reputation.* Paperback ed. Chicago: University of Chicago Press, 1993.

——. *The Problems of Jurisprudence.* Paperback ed. Cambridge, Mass.: Harvard University Press, 1993.

——. *Overcoming Law.* Cambridge, Mass.: Harvard University Press, 1995.

——. *Law and Legal Theory in England and America.* Oxford: Clarendon, 1996.

——. *The Problematics of Moral and Legal Theory.* Cambridge, Mass.: Harvard University Press, Belknap Press, 1999.

——. *Law, Pragmatism and Democracy.* Cambridge, Mass.: Harvard University Press, 2003.

Post, Robert C. *Constitutional Domains: Democracy, Community, Management.* Cambridge, Mass.: Harvard University Press, 1995.

Pound, Roscoe. *An Introduction to the Philosophy of Law.* New Haven, Conn.: Yale University Press, 1954.

Primus, Richard A. *The American Language of Rights.* Cambridge, Mass.: Cambridge University Press, 1999.

Quine, W. V., and J. S. Ullivan. *The Web of Belief.* 2nd ed. New York: Random House, 1978.

Reich, Charles A. *Opposing the System.* New York: Crown, 1995.

Rorty, Richard. *Philosophy and the Mirror of Nature.* Princeton, N.J.: Princeton University Press, 1979.

———. *Consequences of Pragmatism (Essays: 1972–1980).* Minneapolis: University of Minnesota Press, 1982.

———. *Contingency, Irony, and Solidarity.* Cambridge: Cambridge University Press, 1989.

Rosenberg, Jay F. *The Practice of Philosophy: A Handbook for Beginners.* 2nd ed. Englewood Cliffs, N.J.: Prentice-Hall, 1984.

Sandel, Michael J. *Democracy's Discontent: America in Search of a Public Philosophy.* Cambridge, Mass.: Harvard University Press, 1996.

Schlatter, Richard. *Private Property: The History of an Idea.* New York: Russell and Russell, 1973.

Singer, Beth J. *Pragmatism, Rights, and Democracy.* New York: Fordham University Press, 1999.

Sleeper, R. W. *The Necessity of Pragmatism: John Dewey's Conception of Philosophy.* New Haven, Conn.: Yale University Press, 1986.

Smith, John E. *Purpose and Thought: The Meaning of Pragmatism.* New Haven, Conn.: Yale University Press, 1978.

Stone, Geoffrey R., Richard A. Epstein, and Cass R. Sunstein, eds. *The Bill of Rights in the Modern State.* Chicago: University of Chicago Press, 1992.

Strum, Philippa. *Louis D. Brandeis: Justice for the People.* Cambridge, Mass.: Harvard University Press, 1984; reprint, New York: Schocken Books, 1984.

Stuhr, John J. *Genealogical Pragmatism: Philosophy, Experience, and Community.* Albany: State University of New York Press, 1997.

The New York Times. *The Downsizing of America.* New York: Times Books, 1996.

Tiles, J. E. *Dewey.* London: Routledge, 1988.

Tushnet, Mark. *Taking the Constitution Away from the Courts.* Princeton, N.J.: Princeton University Press, 1999.

Watson, Alan. *Failures of the Legal Imagination.* Edinburgh: Scottish Academic Press, 1988.

Weissberg, Richard. *The Failure of the Word.* New Haven, Conn.: Yale University Press, 1984.

West, Cornel. *The American Evasion of Philosophy: A Genealogy of Pragmatism.* Madison: The University of Wisconsin Press, 1989.

White, G. Edward. *Justice Oliver Wendell Holmes: Law and the Inner Self.* Oxford: Oxford University Press, 1993.

White, James Boyd. *Heracles' Bow: Essays on the Rhetoric and Poetics of the Law.* Madison: University of Wisconsin Press, 1985.

Williams, Patricia. *The Alchemy of Race and Rights.* Cambridge, Mass.: Harvard University Press, 1991.

Wolfe, Christopher. *The Rise of Modern Judicial Review: From Constitutional Interpretation to Judge-Made Law.* New York: Basic Books, 1986.

Wolff, Robert Paul. *In Defense of Anarchism.* New York: Harper Torchbooks, 1976.

Young, Iris Marion. *Justice and the Politics of Difference.* Princeton, N.J.: Princeton University Press, 1990.

INDEX

MICHAEL SULLIVAN is Associate Professor of Philosophy at Emory University. He has a J.D. from Yale Law School and a Ph.D. in philosophy from Vanderbilt University. He has taught legal theory and jurisprudence at Emory University Law School and the University of Oregon Law School.

Printed and bound by CPI Group (UK) Ltd, Croydon, CR0 4YY

13/04/2025